D0281632

tracing your
family history

www.thegoodwebguide.co.uk

Dedication

For Maureen, and others, whose enthusiasm for the quest sometimes outstrips the knowledge of where to start or how to follow the clues.

thegoodwebguide

tracing your family history

Caroline and Jonathan Peacock

The Good Web Guide Limited • London

First Published in Great Britain in 2002 by The Good Web Guide Limited
65 Bromfelde Road London SW4 6PP

www.thegoodwebguide.co.uk

©2002 The Good Web Guide Ltd.
Text © 2002 Caroline and Jonathan Peacock

10 9 8 7 6 5 4 3 2 1

A catalogue record for this book is available from the British Library

ISBN 1 903282 33 0

Project editor Karen Fitzpatrick

Printed in Italy by LEGO spa

contents

introduction

We have a friend, to whom this book is dedicated, who is passionately keen to learn more about her family, in terms of who they were, where they lived and what they did. She has embarked on the quest from a very typical starting point, knowing the names of her four grandparents, some of their siblings (her great uncles and aunts), and one or two of her eight great-grandparents.

She has a good knowledge of where to look, geographically, for at least one branch of her family, and she has a certain amount of anecdotal material in the way of hand-me-down stories. To this, she can add a few photographs, some identified more by guesswork than any certainty, one or two letters and a few treasured items said to have belonged to one or another of her ancestors.

Her best characteristic is her boundless enthusiasm and her delight in any new discoveries, however small; but as a family historian it is also her worst characteristic. It leads her into all sorts of dangers, such as jumping too rapidly to conclusions, making wrong connections and not being sufficiently rigorous about checking every source.

Having done a little exploration with our help, she has now begun the painstaking task of building up a true family tree. It sometimes seems unkind to explain to her that the process will take many years, that it will lead to many frustrations when promising lines of enquiry result in dead ends, and that some gaps may never successfully be filled. Happily, she is completely undaunted.

She has recently become aware that there are huge genealogical riches to be explored on the Internet, and that even if the relevant documents cannot be read online (yet), they can at least be identified as existing and therefore can be located. This book is written for her, and for others equally captivated by the search and equally in need of guidance as to how to pursue it.

chapter 01

getting started

You first need to decide what you want to trace. The usual approach is to follow the direct male line. Sooner or later, however, you will run out of direct-line information and may then decide to follow a female or collateral line.

You should assemble any **family-owned documents**, such as birth, marriage and death certificates, certificates of educational achievement, apprenticeships, Service Records, letters, memberships of any organisations, subscriptions, bills, receipts, photos and, of course, wills. Family Bibles may have records in them.

You should then make a list of **all known relatives**, with dates of birth and, if relevant, of marriage and death, recording their relationship to yourself. It is important to identify which are blood relatives and which are only related by marriage.

Living relatives may still own documents, letters and photographs but collecting these may be time-consuming and not all relatives will be as interested as you are. You may have to request **access to family papers** and do the searching yourself. Write in pencil on the back of photographs – it is easy to forget names.

You should now start assembling copies of missing **birth, marriage and death certificates** (see page 35). The value of sending for copies of the certificates is in the detail they provide, which is not available solely from the index, which records only name, place and date.

Noting all details from the certificates, including locations where events took place, occupations, names of witnesses etc. may help you make useful connections later.

There are pitfalls to avoid. The idea that 'owners of the same surname will all be related' is far from true. Every town had occupations like smith, miller, baker or tanner. The suffix 'son' was added to many first names (e.g. Peterson), and every town had a reeve, every shire a sheriff etc.

The assertion 'our name has always been spelt this way' is equally dangerous. Spelling was fluid until the nineteenth century when literacy became widespread, so allow for all possible variant spellings.

Be suspicious of claims like 'we came over with William the Conqueror'. Few families can claim this. Not more than a couple of dozen can prove it. An apparently French surname is certainly no indication.

Also, the belief that 'every family has a coat of arms' is by no means true, though Burke's (see page 108) might like you to think so and will be very happy to charge you for the privilege of concocting your pedigree!

setting objectives

First and foremost, specify your aim. You may wish to find all your own known forebears or, working in the opposite direction, all the known descendants of one identified early ancestor.

You may be collecting all your ancestors and relatives with a specific name (a one-name study) or researching the history of a house and its occupants.

You may choose to restrict your focus to a particular period, to learn about its social history in relation to certain members of your family.

Equally, you may become interested in a defined trade or profession with which your family has been especially connected.

Each of the above is equally valid, but each requires a different type of research using different sources. There is no right or wrong way of setting your aim, but you must identify it clearly – clarity leads to success, while vagueness leads to frustration.

Next, you need to consider how you will present your results. The form in which you will store the information is defined by which of the above aims you have chosen.

When presenting family trees – either of known ancestors or of the descendants of one individual – various formats are available (these are discussed in more detail in the next chapter). Whatever method you choose, expandability is essential. The size of the file you will produce, whether in paper form or stored in your computer, may itself present some problems.

Storing the history of a property or house is likely to be a much simpler matter. Its ownership, whether passing from father to son within a single family, or changing hands at intervals, will remain straightforward, collateral branches being irrelevant. This may prove to be a fascinating quest, linking the property to other families in the area and to historical events.

Using your family history research to learn about the background of a place in which an ancestor lived can be very instructive, leading into many different areas of social history, such as agriculture, industry, the development of a town or district etc.

As an example, in our family we have an ancestor who, having purchased himself a minor French title in 1785, found himself identified as an aristocrat in 1789. He had to flee the country to avoid being guillotined during the French Revolution.

He escaped to sugar estates the family owned in San Domingo where he was murdered only a few years later in a major uprising. That event has recently been chronicled in a book that was a fascinating read, especially since our ancestor was one of the victims.

The investigation of particular trades or professions can lead into equally intriguing areas. Our Parkin and Robinson relatives in and around Appleby were associated with the Post Office, and the more we have discovered about them the more it has become plain that employment within that organisation was very much a family matter, if not a virtual family sinecure.

It is important to decide which route you are taking and what you hope the outcome will be. The random assembling of details seldom works. Your research will be unfocused and you are liable to be dissatisfied.

organising your data

With conventional family tree presentations of the flow-chart type, where the first box on the page leads to two boxes for parents, four for grandparents and so on, it is normal to record only the names, dates of birth and death, and possibly dates of marriage(s).

Even if you have neat handwriting, you will find that you seldom have space for any more detail than this.

The classic downward-facing tree (sometimes termed a 'drop-line tree'), which starts from the earliest identified ancestor and traces all subsequent branches, becomes very wide very quickly.

Similarly, if you work in the opposite direction, creating a backward facing tree to show all the identified forebears of one individual, you will find that the picture widens more slowly but may become very long.

Another popular format is the circular one, where the first individual is presented in the centre, and is surrounded by a succession of rings; the first divided in half to name two parents, the next in four to show grandparents, and so on. After about six or eight generations it becomes quite hard to use this format. The individual compartments in which you are writing become very small.

If you are only recording names this may not matter too much, but if you want to add dates and any other information you will find this pattern restrictive.

A fan-shaped chart can also be used along similar lines to show one half of the family tree.

All of these 'pictorial' trees are reasonably satisfactory, but you are likely to want to record more detailed knowledge about some individuals in the tree. You will need a supplementary data storage system, as a back-up to the basic tree. The most conventional method would be to store this information in files or card indexes.

You need to identify a format that suits your own needs, probably by first selecting one individual with the amount of detail that would satisfy you if applied to others.

It may help to look at bespoke sheets of the sort commercially sold as 'blanks'. These can be obtained, for example, from the Family Records Centre or from your local Family History Society. They offer a succession of compartments into which you can hand-write names and further details as you discover them.

Eventually, of course, you will have to leave gaps. You may be able to name your four grandparents and, with luck and some good research, you will probably be able to identify your eight great-grandparents and even your sixteen great-great-grandparents.

At this point you will very likely be in the mid-nineteenth century and records, such as census returns, will begin to peter out. The quest accordingly becomes more difficult, and you will find that you will be forced to leave some boxes empty. Cross-referencing becomes not only a problem but also an interesting intellectual challenge.

If you approach the matter logically, giving a number to every person in every successive generation (1 for your first individual, 2 and 3 for the parents, 4 to 7 for the grand-parents, then 8 to 15, 16 to 31 and so on) you will soon end up with a massive number of potential records (over a million ancestors by about the year 1500), with some you know nothing about, not even their names. Cross-referencing becomes numerically elaborate if you accommodate all these blank pages or cards.

If you restrict the numbering only to those ancestors you have identified, how will you rearrange the whole set if you unexpectedly manage to fill a gap at a later date? Such questions need to be addressed when you start, because the difficulties they present will only be magnified later if you do not have a clear view of your own system.

The obvious solution is to use a computer programme. Be aware, though, that whichever one you choose, from the simplest to the most sophisticated, it will only actually record-keep in the same manner as described above. You need to imagine it in those terms, as an on-screen version of a typical filing system.

Don't assume that infinite expandability will not be a problem because, although this is one area in which computers normally excel, some genealogy databases restrict the total number of records they can hold.

Cross-referencing, on the other hand, will often be considerably assisted. For example, Family Tree Maker and others will pick up duplicated names and ask you to check whether they refer to the same person.

The programmes have become increasingly ingenious, developing at an impressive rate, no doubt motivated by recognition of a massive potential market. They now offer clever devices such as personal detail 'notepads', relationship calculators and ready-made compartments into which you can 'paste' photographs, either digitally transferred or scanned.

Even so, you may find that the field lengths are too limited for your needs. Some provide their own beginner's guides to genealogy, some enable you to create GEDCOMs (see page 49) and some, like Brother's Keeper, are capable of relating your own records to the historical 'timeline' of the period, both national and international, and producing an indexed book. Generations Grande Suite comes with 15 CD-roms of genealogical data, but be warned, most of what they contain is American.

There is no doubt, therefore, that computer programmes can help, but you need to decide how many 'bells and whistles' you are actually likely to use. It is also worth remembering that you will only ever be able to view what appears on your screen at any one time, and the further 'out' you move the smaller the text will become, eventually to the point of illegibility unless you click selectively to enlarge. You will therefore either be holding a sizeable mental map in your head or you will wish to print out a hard copy version of the tree. Printing out is going to be something you don't want to have to do very often. For instance, a family tree of twenty generations stored in a Family Tree Maker computer programme would, when printed out, cover 54 sheets of A4 paper.

It is impossible to say which programme is the best, especially as new ones keep being produced. We refer you instead to the review in Family Tree Magazine for June 2000. This offers a very comprehensive table, giving you the relevant computer hardware requirements for running each programme, the cost, a basic assessment and a reference for a longer review.

Don't forget that even with a computer, physical storage space will still remain relevant. Over time you will assemble an amazing collection of papers, certificates, maps, photographs and similar objects, not to mention reference books, and you need somewhere to keep all of them too!

joining family history societies

It is important to join societies, partly for access to experts who can offer advice and guidance, and partly for introductions to people who, reassuringly, share your madness.

The most important society to join is unquestionably your local Family History Society. Membership typically costs under £10 per year.

It doesn't matter if you are not living in an area that has been especially connected with your family in the past, because your local FHS will still have the benefit of being physically close.

It will hold meetings and run events and it almost certainly has assets, in the shape of books and documents, that you can consult or borrow, and will be relevant not only locally but also further afield. Its members can advise you about what to do, where to look and how to advance your research.

Research will soon take you away from home. Very few people today find that all four of their grandparents were born in the county where they live. The next step is to join FHSs in other counties.

Although all English counties have their own FHSs, you will find that there are also some affiliated societies or groups representing smaller areas, such as London and North Middlesex, West Middlesex etc.

It may be relevant to join for a limited period, if your research is likely to be concentrated in terms of the time you need to spend on it or the extent of information you expect to find.

Many FHS magazines list members prepared to do research free of charge on a swap basis. If you are willing to research in your own locality in exchange for information, this may be a very good way of resolving geographical difficulty.

www.ffhs.org.uk

The Federation of Family History Societies

Formed in 1974, the Federation now has a very extensive website linking you to its 200 or so member societies. **First Steps in Family History** is a well-constructed introduction, using a question and answer format. The signposting around the site, to benefits of membership, the list of members, lists of publications and research services is very clear.

SPECIAL FEATURES

Strays (people located as being 'from' or connected with somewhere other than their place of normal residence) Very useful and often under-used, as well as **Soldier Ancestors** and **Adopted Persons**.

1901 Census Online A major feature about the disastrous launch of this census, describing its failure to cope with the number of 'hits' and the poor quality of some of the transcribed data.

Internal Links Gives access to Welsh and Irish FHSs, as well as all the English ones, and there are also good links to FHSs abroad. Visiting individual societies' web pages, you will find that they all offer lists of their own publications, some readable online. Most publish regular bulletins or newsletters, again often in an online form. A complete list of all FHS members' publications should shortly be available on CD-rom.

Current projects include:

The National Burial Index A massive effort is being undertaken by FHSs to register details of burials nationwide, deliberately to complement the IGI (see page 30), which records births and marriages but not deaths. The National Burial Index is already partly available on CD, listing 5 million names.

National Inventory of War Memorials In conjunction with the Imperial War Museum.

www.safhs.org.uk

The Scottish Association of Family History Societies

The Scottish Association, formed in 1986, naturally has a smaller website but it covers similar general ground and offers good onward links.

www.gendocs.demon.co.uk/ lon-fhs.html

Gendocs

Gendocs lists all London FHSs here, most usefully.

the society of genealogists

The Society, affectionately known as SoG, is a charity whose aim is to support family historians in their research.

SoG constitutes an amazing source of information, offering by far the best genealogical library in the country, containing many bequests of personal collections and similar deposits.

It is geographically located in Goswell Road, London EC1, and to make full use of its great riches you need to go in person. You will find that it has a massive card index of its holdings, in addition to material on microfiche and CD-rom.

You can go as a non-member paying an hourly or daily rate (currently £12.00) but you will probably find that annual membership is worthwhile. Reduced rates used to be available to those living outside London but regrettably this is no longer the case.

If you want to take genealogy really seriously, gaining qualifications as a researcher with a view to earning a living, for example, membership of SoG will be a prerequisite.

www.sog.org.uk

The Society of Genealogists

It is an oddity that what would appear to be basic introductory material in this website, such as where to visit the society, how to become a member and what information is available online, is presented a third of the way down the homepage. Above, you will find **Latest News, Library, Bookshop, Lectures & Other Events, Family History Fairs** and a new section, entitled **English Origins**, which is progressively offering the Boyd's Marriage Indexes online. A condensed index in the margin would consequently be helpful.

SPECIAL FEATURES

The Library contains Parish Registers (over 9,000), County Records, Poll Books and Directories as well as a great deal of general material about education, the professions, the services, the peerage and religious denominations. Do make use of the 'Before Coming to the Library' advice which tells you how to prepare in order to make a visit more productive.

The Bookshop has an increasingly important online presence, with an 'every word' search facility.

The Society runs an excellent programme of lectures, courses, visits to places of interest and other events, although regrettably few take place outside of London.

Projects include the volunteer transcription of the Vicar General Marriage Licences between 1694 and 1850: a major undertaking already part available in book and microfiche form, and to be published online.

The Society Online You will find the two mailing lists run by the society, one a Discussion List restricted to members and the other a News & Information List open to all. Also listed here are the Society's two regular publications, **Genealogists' Magazine**, which takes a fairly technical approach, and **Computers in Genealogy**. Current issues are available to members only, though past issues of the latter magazine become readable online.

General Under this heading you will find the **Links** section, which may prove very useful as a shortcut to a good list of other relevant organisations – saving you the effort of bookmarking them all separately.

If you can go to London, there are two 'musts', the Family Record Centre (see page 31) for highly specific things such as wills, BDMs and Census returns – and for anything else SoG.

Ireland, Scotland and Wales

Selected in this section are some of the best Irish, Scottish and Welsh websites, allowing the researcher to explore further.

Most of the holdings of the Public Record Office of Ireland were destroyed in 1922 and much primary material was thereby lost. However, it is too simplistic to state that all Irish records were burnt.

Ireland's other archives have been extensively trawled for surviving records and numerous treasures have come to light, including many contemporary transcriptions of documents formerly held by the PRO.

You should not despair as soon as you discover that you have Irish ancestry. Remember that you may also need to research in Northern Ireland where records are more complete. See PRONI (right).

Scotland was for so many centuries an independent country, with its own record holdings, therefore Scottish records are well documented and easily accessible.

Research can often be pursued successfully in Edinburgh – so good are the holdings there – avoiding the need to travel extensively around the country. The passionate devotion to family fostered (and in the past sometimes violently expressed) by the clan system has also contributed to the richness of Scottish archives.

While both Ireland and Scotland are already well served by genealogical and family history websites, the same is not yet true of Wales.

In general, however, it can be assumed that the holdings in England will be paralleled by those in Wales, so that the process of research will be similar even if the internet sources are not yet so extensive.

http://bubl.ac.uk/link/i/irish-history.htm
BUBL link 5:15 – Irish History

The emphasis of this page, sited within the BUBL network, is on history rather than specifically family history. You can find out about Celtic art and culture, the Great Irish Famine and the Troubles.

www.nationalarchives.ie
The National Archives of Ireland

Holdings include Census Returns, BMDs and Wills, among other extensive records. Little is readable online but this site will help you plan a visit.

www.ifhf.org
The Irish Family History Forum

This US-based site will be of interest to those with North American/Irish connections.

www.ireland.anglican.org/library/libroots.html
Library of the Church of Ireland

Although of limited scope, this site introduces the Library's holdings, including registers from 600 parishes in the Republic.

http://proni.nics.gov.uk
The Public Record Office of Northern Ireland

Unquestionably the most important source for research into Northern Ireland's records.

www.gro-scotland. gov.uk
General Register Office for Scotland

Scottish births, marriages, deaths, divorces, adoptions and Census records are all lodged here, so this is an important starting point. Use of the 1901 Census is currently being digitised; involves charges, as does use of the excellent Scots Origins link.

www.scotsorigins.com
Scots Origins

The official government resource for Scottish genealogy.

www.nas.gov.uk
National Archives of Scotland

The Family History section of the National Archives of Scotland, which is otherwise about the history of Scotland, offers excellent advice to researchers.

www.scotsgenealogy.com
The Scottish Genealogy Society

Contact and location details are given, with a brief outline of library holdings.

www.geo.ed.ac.uk/home/scotland/genealogy.html
Tracing your Scottish Ancestry

Offers onward links to other web pages, especially about clans and tartans.

www.edinburgh.gov.uk/libraries
Edinburgh City Libraries

This website has a History Sphere link, from which you need to scroll to the right to find the Family History section.

www.rcahmw.org.uk/links.shtml
RCAHMW

This is where to start if researching in Wales. Under Sites and Monuments, Archives, Family History Societies, Historical Societies, Museums, Universities and

General Welsh Links, you will find a mass of relevant material.

www.llgc.org.uk
The National Library of Wales

The website for the National Library of Wales can be found at this address.

genforums and message boards

This area of internet genealogy and family history should be explored with caution – you cannot necessarily assume that the contributors will have worked with true investigative or academic rigour.

Having delivered that warning, however, it is important to make use of this rather chaotic area of the World Wide Web. You may discover something very worthwhile.

It is entirely possible that an unknown relative is already well into tracing the history of your own family. Therefore, making contact with him or her would offer you a massive shortcut in your own research.

If you do make such a discovery you need, tactfully, to check the sources your informant has used. Good researchers document every source as they go along and should not be offended by your wish to have chapter and verse for every connection.

Don't confuse one-name studies and personal family trees. People creating one-name studies undertake to collect every known occurrence in the world, past or present, of a particular surname.

Such data may be valuable in helping avoid 'wrong' branches of your personal family line, and may become fascinating for other reasons, e.g. the geographical migration of certain family names or associations between certain names and professions.

If interested in this sort of research you should join the Guild of One-Name Studies (GOONS) at **www.one-name.org,** whose site also offers good onward links.

Seeking out online versions of personal family trees which explore the descent of a single family line may be of more use to you. These need to be recorded in internet-usable form and the normal way of doing this is to present them as GEDCOMs (see page 49).

Name-searching, by means of simply typing your name into the search engine facility of a name-search website, is a pretty haphazard art. For a start, the majority of websites that entice you with offers of millions of names are, in fact, US-based.

Many families, of course, do have North American connections and if this is your own case you may strike lucky.

On the other hand, if no members of your family have ever emigrated across the Atlantic, it is fairly unlikely that anyone over there will be researching your particular family tree.

The best-known examples of such US-based name-searching websites are:

Rootsweb
www.rootsweb.com

Ancestry.com
www.ancestry.com

GENDEX
www.gendex.com

Gensource.com
www.gensource.com

They all exist only as internet resources, and they are all massive in scope. They tend to be cluttered and jazzy in appearance, a style you will soon recognise as typically American, but their onward links may be well worth exploring.

Mailing lists and message boards, especially those in the UK, may be helpful, particularly if you want to interact with other enthusiasts.

There are plenty of topic-specific mailing lists, easily found through a good search engine such as Google (**www.google. co.uk**).

Any message you submit will be posted to all other members of a mailing list group, and you will also receive all messages posted by others. You may like to scan some of the past discussion points before deciding to join.

Newsgroups are similarly topic-related and you will probably need a newsreader in order to use them (normally downloadable from the web).

Within the UK there are several local information websites that are hosted under broad-based or universal umbrellas. Their URLs are prefixed by such terms as **www.communigate**, **www.fish4** and **www.thisis** followed by the location, and some of these contain family history areas.

basic information:
starting to build a family tree

If you test 'family history' in Google you currently get over three-and-a-half-million hits.

You still get over 700,000 even if you restrict your search to the UK (one of the invaluable facilities of **www.google. co.uk**).

From this bewildering starting point, how on earth should you proceed?

Even complete beginners in family history research can make use of the Internet to their advantage.

There are are several general-purpose websites that offer first-class tutorials and advice for the newcomer.

The following are among the best:

www.genuki.org.uk

The UK and Ireland Genealogical Service

No matter whether you are a total beginner or a very experienced family historian, GENUKI has something for you.

SPECIAL FEATURES

Getting Started in Genealogy One of the best online tutorials available and will help you get going. Apparent offers of good research material by other websites often transfer back to pages within GENUKI.

www.bbc.co.uk/history/community/family

BBC Family History

For those who like a very accessible presentation, this may be more appealing than the rather staid approach of GENUKI

and, though nothing like as extensive, the advice it gives is good and reliable. It is hardly surprising that this website is picture-rich, given its provenance, but that can make it slow to load. There are some unexpected corners to explore here, such as the 'mugshots' of Victorian criminals. Also, drawing on past BBC programme successes such as 'Roots' and 'Bloodties', it offers a strong introduction to African-Caribbean family history.

www.cyndislist.com

Cyndis List of Genealogy Sites on the Internet

Yes, it's American and it's big – but it's incredibly good, too. Cyndi Howells lists nearly 130,000 genealogy links, with everything from starter tutorials to very specialist resources. The great joy here is the clarity of presentation, not a quality one might pick out as typical of many American websites. Cyndi and her husband, Mark, who handles the British area of the website, have done a wonderfully logical job of sorting a mass of genealogical material into a conveniently usable form.

www.wilshawi.freeserve.co.uk /fh_link.html
Family History on the Web

Ian Wilshaw keeps a long list here of family history material, including a host of useful links both to local resources in the UK and to family history material abroad, notably in Australia, Canada and the US.

www.familyrecords.gov.uk
Family Records.gov.uk

This is not the Family Records Centre (see page 31), though a link from this site does go there. It's more of an umbrella for other websites already described, and not a very good one at that.

www.englishorigins.com
English Origins

English Origins is part of the larger Origins.net website, whose transcribers first put Scottish records online, and who are now doing the same for some of the Society of Genealogists' material. Use **Helps and Tips** before getting carried away with testing the **Free Surname Search,** which is only fully free to SoG members. Otherwise, you search the surname list free and then pay at a rate of £6.00 for 48 hours to download records. Increasingly, details of marriages and wills are available for online reading.

Unfortunately there is not space to explore in detail the ways in which you can make day-to-day use of the Internet more efficient and cost effective. For that purpose we refer you to the companion volume, the *Good Web Guide: Genealogy*. Recently published in a much-updated, much-expanded second edition, it is also newly available in paperback. It is a worthwhile investment even for those who already own the first edition. Overlap between that book and this one is deliberately kept to a minimum.

family records centre

The FRC is a comparatively new establishment (including the building it occupies) in Myddelton Street, London EC1. It was set up in 1997 as a joint service between the Public Record Office (PRO) and the Office for National Statistics (ONS). It brings together the census records and some will information which used to be in the PRO in Portugal Street and Chancery Lane, with lists of births, marriages, deaths and adoptions, which were in the General Register Office in St Catherine's House. It also contains the IGI (see page 31) on CD-rom rather than microfiche, which otherwise only exists in some Mormon Family History Centres and very few other places.

Standing not far from Kings Cross Station, the FRC is conveniently close to the London Metropolitan Archives (see page 45) and not far from the Society of Genealogists (see page 20). It is extremely well laid out and user friendly, with a vast array of microfilm and microfiche readers, and the staff are exceptionally helpful.

However, it has a limited range of books and maps, and for parish information SoG is better. It is worth noting though that non-conformist (as opposed to parish) registers are lodged at the FRC. For straightforward genealogical research or family-tree building the FRC is unsurpassed.

If you are visiting in person, you can simply walk in and start using the centre's facilities free of charge and without the need to pre-book. For those unable to go to London, or who simply prefer to 'visit' by using the Internet at home, the following three websites are the way in:

www.familyrecords.gov.uk

FRC

This rather inadequate gateway is one point of entry, though the FRC itself suggests that it may be as easy to select a more direct route, depending on whether you are interested principally in census information or BDMs. They advise the following:

www.pro.gov.uk

The Public Record Office

This is where you should address general enquiries (also by telephone: 0208 392 5300) and look for census information from 1841 to 1891. What you can expect to glean from census returns is explained in much greater detail on page 39. The much-vaunted project to digitise the 1901 Census, only recently released under the one-century-later rule, has been a spectacular failure because the website immediately collapsed under the weight of hits. It has not yet been repaired.

www.ons.gov.uk

The Office for National Statistics

The Office is geographically located at Southport on Merseyside, so is remote from London (though it can be telephoned on 0151 471 4800). Via this internet link, however, you can search the lists for your ancestors in BDM records and then, as with a visit to the FRC in person, order the relevant certificates. Divorce records 1858–1958 are now available on microfilm, too.

Most of the records you will be consulting, such as the Census Returns and Wills, Letters of Administration and Death Duty Registers, will be found on easily readable microfilm. These can be read in full, as opposed to the BDM material, which simply indexes (in massive ledgers) what certificates exist and can be ordered. For an explanation of the value of obtaining the actual certificates see page 35.

the international genealogical index

www.familysearch.com

The International Genealogical Index

Popularly known as the Mormon Index, this immense and still growing database has been created by members of the Church of Jesus Christ of the Latter-day Saints, based in Salt Lake City, Utah.

Since they baptise their ancestors, posthumously, into the Mormon faith, some record holders (in the UK, parish priests) have refused access. Most have permitted the transcription of records, creating the world's largest, free genealogical database.

The IGI indexes by country and then county, birth (or more accurately baptismal) and marriage entries abstracted from parish registers. It once contained no entries of deaths, although some are now being added.

In the past, if you knew in what parish to seek an event or entry, it might be relatively easy to find it. If it was not there, however, and in the absence of any surname indexes, you had no idea where else to look. You could only assume that people might not have moved far, and successively search every parish record, moving outwards geographically. For example, if a couple weren't married in a parish, where were they baptised? That knowledge might give you a useful hint.

The wonderful advantage of the IGI is that it does index by surname within every county. You can therefore search the whole of England, for example, in only 54 searches.

When using it, however, you must recognise two great weaknesses. The first is that it is far from complete. Although some 60-million entries have so far been recorded in the UK (one of the most comprehensively covered countries), some counties' parish records are still not fully transcribed. If you fail to find the entry you seek, you have no way of knowing whether this is because it hasn't been transcribed or because it doesn't exist.

The other major failing is that the transcription has been done manually, so there are many inaccuracies. It should therefore only ever be used as an indication of where to check the primary reference.

Spellings, for example, are a major issue. The Index tries to bring variant spellings together but you should still use common sense to check more widely.

The Index is available on microfiche in many County Record Offices, on the Internet and on CD-rom in Mormon Family History Centres and some other places such as the FRC (see page 31).

On microfiche you choose the county you are interested in and select the fiche that gives the alphabetical surname entry you want. The data is then listed by county, surname, first name, date and event.

In the CD-rom version, you type in the name and the country of interest, selecting from a choice of fields if you wish, such as county or date period. This is more akin to using the Internet (which is itself well explained in the website, including how to use the batch numbers system to find further family members).

In the case of baptisms the Index will probably give the father's name, and sometimes the mother's. Marriages usually record spouses and both always give the date of the entry and the parish. It is up to you to go back to the original document to find out more. For example, some clergymen also gave birth dates when making baptism entries.

The IGI is a vast and valuable starting point for building your family tree but it is not, on its own, the whole answer.

births, marriages and deaths – also burials and obituaries

'BDMs' is an expression that does not just belong to civil registration; because the earliest registrations are found in Parish Records, and these are explained in more detail elsewhere (see page 43).

The 1689 Toleration Act allowed marriage in churches other than the Church of England. This means that prior to that date you only need to consult Anglican records, whereas thereafter you should check those of the Non-Conformist churches, such as the Methodists, the Quakers etc. Hardwick's Marriage Act of 1754 set out the details that had to be recorded and provided a blank ledger to be filled in.

This remained the format of information up to July 1837 when civil registration was introduced. It became a legal requirement that all BDMs were registered. These records were initially held at Somerset House, then at St Catherine's House in the Strand and are now in the Family Records Centre in Myddelton Street, London.

They are in the format of indexes by the quarter, so there are four for each year. Some are presented as a typed index and some are still handwritten.

Remember, when using the early indexes, that failing to find the individual sought does not mean he or she does not exist. Civil registration was not universally observed.

You should also be careful to check spellings, as these can be variable.

When you get a certificate it has certain information on it. A birth certificate gives details of the place and date of birth, name ('if any!') of the child and its sex; the name and surname of the father; the name, surname and maiden surname of the mother; the occupation of the father; the signature, description and residence of the informant; when the birth was registered and the signature of the registrar.

A marriage certificate says when the couple were married, giving names and surnames of the bride and groom, their ages (often recorded simply as 'full', meaning over 21), their condition (bachelor, spinster etc.), their rank or profession, residence at time of marriage, father's names and surnames, and father's rank or profession. The place of marriage is given below. At the bottom of the page are the signatures of the couple and those of the witnesses.

Don't ignore these, as they may provide confirmation of things that have hitherto been guesswork. For example, other family members were often used as witnesses.

Death certificates record when and where someone died, the name and surname, sex, age, occupation and cause of death. The record is completed by the signature, description and residence of the informant, giving the date of registration and the signature of the registrar.

The age at death is often most useful, as that throws you back to a date of birth, though this may only be a clue as the age recorded is not necessarily accurate. Also, don't forget that a year comprises 12 months; so, for example, a person dying in 1890, aged 90, may actually have been born at some date in 1799 but have died before their 91st birthday.

When ordering certificates, it is cheaper to apply in person than by post and, if your family has long lived in the same area it is also cheaper to use a Local Register Office than the General Register Office in Southport, Lancashire.

Requests accompanied by the correct index reference cost less than those without (currently £8.00 instead of £11.00). Copies of certificates may take several days or even weeks to come. See also the UK BDM Exchange (page 142).

divorce records

Under the rule of the Catholic Church, divorce was not permitted. The only possible end of a valid marriage came with death. Divorce was only ever granted on the ground that the marriage was in some way invalid.

England did not have a law permitting divorce until 1858 and was the last Protestant country in Europe to pass such a law by some considerable time.

The alternatives to divorce were separation, whether private or formalised, desertion and, in a few cases, the extraordinary resort of 'wife sale' (the theme that Thomas Hardy took for his novel *The Mayor of Casterbridge*). Bigamous marriages, in a situation where divorce was so difficult, were common.

Indexes to divorce records 1858–1958 are in the Public Record Office with corresponding case files. Before 1858, some records survive and can be searched, though these are by no means complete. Two PRO leaflets are available online (see page 38). PRO staff are able to do research on your behalf, at a rate of £15 per hour (minimum 1 hour).

'Road to Divorce: England 1530–1987' (studies in marriage litigation in the Court of Arches and the London Consistory Court) by Lawrence Stones was published in 1990 and is a major text for anyone wanting to study the history of divorce.

If you enter the abbreviated title 'Road to Divorce' in Amazon and click the 'Reviews' link you will get an excellent synopsis of the book, along with a couple of quotes from Christopher Hibbert and Claire Tomalin. This is a very convenient way of obtaining a synopsis of books and can, of course, be applied in other situations.

Another scholarly book on the same topic, though taking a wider European overview, is 'Untying the Knot: A Short History of Divorce' by Roderick Phillips.

http://catalogue.pro.gov.uk/Leaflets/ri2288.htm

The Public Record Office explains in some detail the law before 1858 when legal divorce was first introduced.

www.pro.gov.uk/research/easysearch/divorce.htm

The Public Record Office provides this very simplified page directing you to some divorce record holdings.

www.nas.gov.uk/miniframe/fact_sheet/divorce.pdf

The National Archives of Scotland offer a page here explaining the slight differences in the law affecting Scotland. The Registrar General keeps a register of divorces granted by Scottish courts (see www.groscotland.gov.uk/grosweb/grosweb.nsf/pages/leaflet1).

http://freespace.virgin.net/owston.tj/divorce.htm

Timothy J. Owston of York often provides useful individual pages on topics of family history interest and this is a good example, simply entitled 'Divorce'. It ends with some information about where records are held and a brief supplementary reading list.

www.royal.gov.uk/output/Page19.asp

This 'History of the Monarchy' article gives a clear account of one of the most famous divorces in English history, that of King Henry VIII from his first wife, Catherine of Aragon.

www.shu.ac.uk/emls/emlsweb.html
Early Modern Literary Studies offers some very interesting, though wordy and not very easy to read transcriptions of the debate regarding divorce that was conducted in the seventeenth century. To find these, click on 'Milton' and then on 'Electronic Transcriptions of Miltons Divorce Tracts'.

www.waters.demon.co.uk/lfbigamy.htm
'In Good Faith and Truthful Ignorance – Researching Bigamy' is the summary of a fascinating talk given by Peter Park in January 2002 at the London and South Branch of the Lancashire Family History and Heraldry Society.

www.isle-of-man.com/manxnotebook/
famhist/vo7n2.htm#54
Isle of Man Family History Society Journal, Volume vii, no 2, April 1985, contains a transcript of an actual divorce decree granted in 1637.

the census

The first national Census was taken on 10 March 1801, as the result of an instruction from the government to the Registrar General. Censuses were taken every ten years thereafter, except in 1941.

The object was to record each person resident in every property (in England, Scotland, Wales, Channel Islands, Isle of Man and Royal Navy) on that night. This means that people away from home on the particular date of the Census are recorded at wherever they were staying rather than in their normal domicile.

This system has the virtue of recording each individual only once, whereas the most recent Census, taken in 2001, has instead opted for recording any person 'who usually lives' in a given property.

As a result of this change a person can potentially be recorded twice. For example, a student could have been recorded twice, once at a term-time address and once by the parents at home.

The earliest Census records have not been preserved. They were, anyway, only a head-count. The first one of any practical use is 1841 which was was carried out on 7 June.

The detail contained in the 1841 Census is fairly limited in that it asked name, age (ages below 15 were exact, but older ages were rounded down to the nearest five years), occupation and whether the person had been born in the county or not. The record is handwritten and its state of preservation is sometimes poor. You will find that parts of it are very difficult to read.

It is, however, still worth persisting because, given that it is recording people alive in 1841, some of these people were born well back into the previous century, which may help you take another step back in time. As the difficulty of locating people is one that always besets ancestor-hunters, this makes the Census particularly helpful.

The Census carried out on 30 March 1851 is more use in that it names the specific place of each person recorded as well as dates of birth. It also gives the relationship of each person to the head of the family, with exact ages.

Any Census may be viewed in a County Record Office (those which have a holding for their county) and nationally in the Family Records Centre in Myddelton Street, London.

The Census itself was never indexed, merely presented in the order in which the census taker happened to walk his route. This means that consulting it in its original form can be a tediously lengthy process.

Two subsequent forms of index have in some cases been created, listing either locations by address or people by surname. Indexing of this nature is partial and has been carried out by many different bodies, such as Family History Societies. Once you can identify the Census year and the location in which you are interested, you should then approach the relevant FHS to see if such indexing has been done. The Family Records Centre also holds copies of those indexes that have been created, which you may find a helpful shortcut.

The Mormons have done a wonderful job of putting onto CD-rom the whole of the national Census for 1881, and for 1851 the counties of Devon, Norfolk and Warwick only. Increasingly, however, you find that local FHSs are also putting them into CD format, for example Gloucestershire, 1851. This method of presentation is fantastic because it is so fully and rapidly searchable.

Separate from the national Census, you may occasionally be lucky enough to find fragments of other earlier censuses. For example, the Westmorland Court of Quarter Sessions decided to take a census of that county in 1787. If you find one of these for your area, you are fortunate indeed.

All the major genealogical websites provide information about the 1901 and other Censuses. You should consult the websites of the **Society of Genealogists** (see page 20), **the Family Records Centre** (see page 31), **the IGI** (see page 33), and **the Public Record Office** (at www.pro.gov.uk).

http://web.ukonline.co.uk/sheila.jones/ceninfo.htm

Sheila Jones has a useful Census-dedicated section here within her Pedigrees and People of the UK website.

For Scottish and Irish Census records, try GROS, the General Register Office for Scotland, and PRONI, the Public Record Office for Northern Ireland (for both see page 23).

In addition, try: **www.scotlandsclans.com/census.htm**.

When it comes to the most recently released Census, for 1901, and the most recently taken Census, in 2001, the following website is helpful and is also part of the PRO:

www.statistics.gov.uk/census2001
The Office of National Statistics' website can be explored here for details of the current Census form, a specimen of which is online. If you click the Census Background link there is good historical information about Censuses past and present.

The data recorded by the Census is always treated as confidential for 100 years, so the newest release, of course, is 1901. If, within this same website, you click Useful Links and scroll down to 1901 Census Records you will call up a page headed 'Sorry, the 1901 Census website is currently being tested'. As we write, the opportunity to read the 1901 Census online seems as distant as ever. Microform copies are, however, available in some County Record Offices, though not in the Family Records Centre.

If you type the words 'failure 1901 census online' into Google, you will be offered a host of websites raging against the abject failure of the attempt to make the 1901 Census available for reading on the Internet.

A spokesman for QinetiQ, the company awarded the £7-million contract to provide this service, was quoted soon after the launch date, 2 January 2002, as saying: 'The site was designed for an average of 1.2-million hits per day but there is an average of 1.2 million hits per hour and it's not letting up.'

They should have expected this, however, given that the Ellis Island website in the US, handled 50-million hits in its first day. The clearest account is probably in the published draft letter to MPs from the Federation of Family History Societies at: **www.ffhs.org. uk/LetterMP.htm**.

The PRO publishes a paperback book called *Making Use of the Census* by Susan

Lumas, and the Stationery Office offers similar help with *Making Sense of the Census* by Edward Higgs.

parish records

The family historian will find that very few parishes (under 700 out of over 11,000) have records going back before 1550. Parish Records started being officially kept in England in 1538 at the behest of Thomas Cromwell. He was secretary to the King (and had earlier been Vicar General) and he had visited the Low Countries (today The Netherlands) where he had observed their record system.

Initially there was considerable public resistance because people suspected that this was likely to be the basis of a new form of taxation, and it was not until the reign of Queen Elizabeth I that it became universal.

Towards the end of the sixteenth century Queen Elizabeth decreed that every parish should also send a copy to its diocese, and these documents became known as the Bishops Transcripts.

During Cromwell's Commonwealth in the seventeenth century many vicars lost their livings for not adhering to Puritan principles, and the replacement incumbents were often less well regulated and less rigorous in their record-keeping. There are, therefore, noticeably more gaps during this period.

From 1660 onwards, however, the situation improved and, while some records have since been lost in instances of flood or fire, you can normally hope to find them. The first place to look is in the relevant County or City Record Office.

The actual records were handwritten by the vicar, who sometimes made notes and then used these later to complete the register. Some of these records are on pieces of parchment where you can see that he had to write around holes in the leather. Any supplementary information that was noted down depended on the whim of the vicar, sometimes recording the actual date of birth as well as of baptism, and indeed sometimes giving the occupation of the father.

A few clergymen also took the opportunity to note down major events in the Parish, such as the church being struck by lightning. Hardwick's Marriage Act of 1754, as we have seen, regularised the information that had to be provided but even after that date some vicars still chose to add extra information.

Today the International Genealogical Index provides a massive database of Parish Records. This aids the search by referring you to a source, though it does not give you any indication of what data you may find if you consult the original record. Eventually the sources of information available to the genealogist are supplemented by civil registration, which began in 1837.

The first port of call for anyone wanting to use the Internet to research Parish Records is GENUKI, the UK and Ireland Genealogical Service (see also pages 22–25). This is found at:

www.genuki.org.uk
The introductory material provided here for those new to genealogy or family history is among the best. The search engine facility is simple to use and is effective. For example, inputting a village name and the words 'parish records' produces several quotations taken from records of various dates, followed by figures for the population at different periods, a description of the parish church and details of where its Registers are held (the County Record Office) as well as advising of other sources to consult.

A very useful page within this normally well organised website is found at **www. genuki.org.uk/big/LatinNotes.html**, where Alison Ring has posted her experience of trying, with limited knowledge, to understand Latin in Parish Records. Tracking down this page by any means other than typing the URL given here may prove difficult.

www.sog.org.uk/vg/vicgen.htm

The Vicar-General Marriage Licence Index is held by the Society of Genealogists (whose transcribers, having completed that task, are now working on The Faculty Office Marriage Licence Index). This provides an index to the surnames recorded in the marriage licences issued by the office of the Vicar General of the Archbishop of Canterbury for the period 1694 to 1850.

Please note that any Parish Registers you cannot manage to track down in the County Record Offices may also be held in transcribed form by the Society of Genealogists (whose main website is described on pages 20–21).

www.familia.org.uk

The Familia website, which is chiefly an introduction to family history material held in libraries throughout the UK and Ireland, offers a brief and clear explanation of what Parish Registers are under its Sources link.

www.englishorigins.com

A free surname search within the Boyd's Marriage Indexes 1538–1840 is available at the English Origins website, though actually downloading the records themselves costs £6.00. This permits 48 hours of use with the collection of up to 150 records. Information about Marriage Licence Allegations is also found in this website.

www.cityoflondon.gov.uk

The City of London Corporation owns the London Metropolitan Archives, which can be accessed here via a remarkably tortuous route, clicking sequentially on Leisure & Heritage, Libraries, Archives, Museums & Galleries and then London Metropolitan Archives. An alternative route is to use the fuller URL, **www.cityoflondon.gov.uk/ applications/family-research/index.htm**.

The London Generations link eventually offers you a searchable database which, while the records themselves are not readable online, will tell you whether a visit to the Archives (near the Family Records Centre in London EC1) might be worthwhile. Parish Registers for all London parishes are held.

http://members.netscapeonline.co.uk/prtsoc/index.html
Should you become fascinated by the whole business of transcribing parish records, you might like to apply to join the Parish Register Transcription Society. Its rather reticent website is available here and the project is a worthy one, even if the records transcribed so far are limited to those counties where the participants have personal links.

http://freereg.rootsweb.com
More extensive in reach is the FreeREG Project, hosted by Rootsweb. The objective is the transcription of Parish Registers and most British counties have identified county co-ordinators for this project.

www.jodenoy.clara.net/genbooks/main.htm
Jodenoy books specialise in genealogy titles and you can find the titles of currently published and in-print Parish Registers (about 50) through a link within Amazon.

http://hometown.aol.com/rjcindex/trueflare.html
In this personal page, entitled Trueflare Ltd., Robert J. Cottrell is principally interested in watermen along the Thames. As a result he offers for sale the Thames & Medway Riverside Parish Registers on microfiche.

published genealogies

Published genealogies are often merely found as family trees within books on more general topics, which may be historical or topographical in approach rather than strictly genealogical. Some entire books, however, are devoted to the record of a particular family and you may be lucky enough to find one that relates to your own ancestry. The problem is how do you discover that such a book exists?

One source is *The Genealogist's Guide* by George W. Marshall, first published in 1879 and reprinted in 1967 by the Genealogical Publishing Company of Baltimore.

J.B. Whitmore's *A Genealogical Guide* extended the process to 1953, and this was followed by *The Genealogist's Guide* by Geoffrey B. Barrow (1977). These books are available in many libraries, and use the format of indexing by surname and then listing relevant publications. After that, you need to track down those publications, usually in libraries, since many are no longer in print, and dig out the references.

Pre-dating both of these, there is the less-known *An Index to Printed Pedigrees* by Charles Bridger, published in 1867 (reprinted in paperback 1987). His system is slightly different, listing the publications by county and cross-referencing to the named families.

Two other books that will be of use are T.R. Thomson's *Catalogue of British Family Histories,* 3rd edition, 1976 and J.P.S. Ferguson's *Scottish Family Histories*, 2nd edition, 1986. These both list families for whom histories in book form are known to exist.

Burke's *Peerage* and *Extinct Peerage* are two important sources for titled families (see page 116). Walford's *County Families* was really an attempt to compete with Burke's other main title, *Landed Gentry* (see page 108). It was first published in 1860, and ran through some fifty annual editions up to 1910. It is always worth checking, as it sometimes contains a family not covered in Burke, although it lacks the depth of Burke in terms of detail.

There are immense numbers of published genealogies available and the Society of Genealogists Library holds several hundred, all meticulously catalogued as 'Printed Pedigrees'.

Remember that in consulting any of these you are at the mercy of the compiler and should be wary of accepting their accuracy without checking references.

www.sog.org.uk/cig/index.html
This introduces the Genealogical Research Directory, published as part of *Computers in Genealogy* by the Society of Genealogists. Use the Online Articles & Reviews link to reach the relevant page. You will find the Directory towards the bottom. It is now available on CD-rom.

www.ffhs.co.uk/shop/pages/raymond.htm
One of the most important sources of printed genealogies is found at this page from within the Federation of Family History Societies' website. The invaluable *British Genealogical Library Guides*, published by the FFHS in association with the author Stuart A. Raymond, are all listed.

www.medievalgenealogy.org.uk
Medieval Genealogy, though restricting itself to that earlier period of British history, gives useful alphabetical lists of families whose pedigrees are available in ready-researched form. It also has a Published Works, Bibliographies and Indexes link.

www.linenhall.com/Collections
This page introduces the collections of the Linen Hall Library, the oldest library in Belfast, and the Genealogy link takes you to a further explanation of relevant holdings.

www.igrsoc.org/index.htm
The Irish Genealogical Research Society is actually in London, in Eaton Square. From its website homepage, select IGRS Library to find out more about what documents and publications it possesses.

www.electricscotland.com
Useful material about Scottish clans and septs of clans is found here, with a very thorough and effective search facility.

GEDCOMs

GEDCOM stands for Genealogical Data Communication and is a system used by many family history software packages to communicate the details of family trees between researchers. It originated as a 'language' or code from the Church of the Latter-day Saints (creators of the IGI) as a means of sharing information between different family history software packages.

The oft-repeated advice about checking sources has to be mentioned here again. For example, there is apparently a method whereby data from the IGI itself can be transported directly into your own personal GEDCOM, but this is not to be recommended. The original records in Parish Registers should always be checked first. The same should be applied to all personal GEDCOM files submitted by other individuals.

A GEDCOM can list, for each individual in the family tree, the name, sex, date and place of birth and death, with further details as you choose. You can decide the amount of information to be displayed about each person. You will find that, once you have learnt your way around, you will probably get quite clever at manipulating the data to fit the space available.

Most genealogy software packages offer a GEDCOM-creation facility and can also accommodate GEDCOMs accepted from other sources. Anyone purchasing new family history software should check that the program is capable of accepting and sending GEDCOM files. There are two principal processes that you should ensure are incorporated, Ged2DBF for converting GEDCOM files to a database, and Ged2HMTL.exe for conversion to a web page.

Many of the major genealogical websites offer GEDCOM-hosting services, though some of these may not offer you enough scope, or space, if you have a lot of material to deposit. For an insight into this area, you may like to consult **www.southfrm.demon. co.uk/Updates/2001_sept.html** where the problems of getting certain websites to accept GEDCOMs are described by one individual user, Tim Powys-Lybbe.

If you are having difficulty transferring data, some users advise sending it in multiple small amounts, rather than as single, very large files.

www.oz.net/~markhow/writing/ gedcom.htm

For a really clear explanation of what a GEDCOM is and how you can get involved, the best tutor, as so often, is Mark Howells, husband of Cyndi of the eponymous 'List'. The above URL is the shortcut to a page by Mark, entitled 'Transforming your GEDCOM Files into Web Pages'.

http://surnameweb.org/help/ conversion.htm

Although a US-based website, Surname Web offers here a 'Which'-style report into the best GEDCOM Conversion Tools. It is equally relevant for UK-based family historians, given that the software programs on offer will be universal.

www.genserv.com

One very well-known GEDCOM-hosting service is GenServ, run by Cliff Manis. It claims to be the first and the largest service of its type. It holds a huge number of GEDCOM databases, submitted by individual family historians worldwide. As a contributor, you can search the entire list and exchange information with other contributors via automated email. The website is very American in style and therefore is probably confusing for a first-time user. However, if you can cope with the repetitions and the many exclamation marks in this site you will most likely find it useful.

www.pennine.demon.co.uk/family/fdoc/
index.html
For those of a technical bent, the
Appendix B: GEDCOM Files link will give a
partial explanation.

monumental
inscriptions

Monumental Inscriptions (MIs) are the last
physical trace we leave – our tombstones.
Churchyard memorials are actually quite
rare before the seventeenth century. The
earliest inscriptions were on wooden
boards, so hardly any of those survive today.

The other early material used was brass and
these, often very ornamental memorials, are
still found in old churches (see **www. mbs-
brasses.co.uk** for more information).
Medieval Genealogy (page 48) also has a
feature on Monumental Brasses on
the Internet.

Monuments are found in larger numbers
from the mid-seventeenth century
onwards, when the wealthier members of
society, if not able to afford to be buried
inside the church with the gentry, could at
least afford to erect a monument outside in
the churchyard.

Later, in the nineteenth century, stone
and slate were more easily and cheaply
transported, and this meant that even
those lower down the social scale could
afford memorials.

Paupers, suicides and criminals, however,
continued to be buried in unmarked graves,
usually outside the consecrated ground of
the churchyard itself.

If you are very lucky you may find that an
ancestor has a tablet or plaque in a church
giving biographical details and, being
indoors, it should be in a good state of
preservation. Inscriptions out of doors,
though sometimes equally informative, are

seldom so immediately readable. Familiarity with the usual Latin terms is useful (see page 145), as Latin continued to be fashionable for memorial inscriptions long after it fell out of common use in church services.

Nowadays many local Family History Societies are recording MIs, both to preserve the information – before weathering and ground clearance removes it forever – and to make that information available for research.

These indexes are available direct from local FHSs (usually on microfiche) or they can be viewed in the Society of Genealogists' Library.

May we offer a word of caution: that great project The National Burial Index, recently published on CD-rom and certainly valuable, does not include MIs. It is based on burial entries from registers in parishes and cemeteries.

www.archivecdbooks.org

The Archive CD Books Project produces, among other CD-roms, *Ancient Funeral Monuments – 1631*, published in 2001. It covers the Dioceses of Canterbury, Rochester, London and Norwich, so is limited in scope. However, if a compact disk can look 'antiquated', this one charmingly does.

Website-owner Rodney Neep is making an increasing number of old books available in this form, and acquires his 'stock' from loans and gifts, as well as from his own purchases. To find the CDs relating specifically to MIs you need to put the words 'monumental inscriptions' into the search box, as they are not automatically listed otherwise.

www.neep.demon.co.uk/mis/index.htm

Rod Neep has another web presence here, introducing the whole topic of recording monumental inscriptions. The notes he provides remain relevant, even though updating of this site does not seem very recent.

www.muir.clara.net/record

Introduced with the words 'Here Lyeth a Decaying Body of Historical Evidence', Transcribing Historical Monuments offers a single, very good page about the topic. There is very useful information about suitable abbreviations that can be used by transcribers working in sometimes adverse weather conditions and a selection of frequently used biblical quotes.

http://members.lycos.co.uk/jimsweb/cemeteries.htm

This Jimsweb web page is a valuable resource, but of limited scope, listing online records of 'Cemetery Inscriptions – England and Wales – Ireland – Scotland'. There is a search facility. 'Jim' is unidentified.

www.scotsgenealogy.com/moninscr.htm

Monumental Inscriptions: A List of Published & Unpublished MIs Held by the Scottish Genealogy Society. This is a list of titles, available at very reasonable prices.

commonwealth war graves commission and other world war records

www.cwgc.org

The Commonwealth War Graves Commission maintains war graves and memorials (and some non-war graves) of those who died in the two World Wars around the world. The 'Services' link explains the CWGC's remit and the limitations of its ability to do research. This remains, however, very much the first place in which to research a wartime casualty.

The idea for the Commission came from Sir Fabian Ware who, in 1914, was shocked by the failure to record the graves of fallen servicemen. In later years he worked tirelessly to persuade foreign governments to allow the Commission to record graves and tend cemeteries. He also became involved in discussions about the architecture for war memorials, the horticultural aspects of cemetery care and all matters regarding the keeping of wartime records.

The 1.7-million men and women who died are commemorated in 150 countries and at some 23,000 locations, so the task of the CWGC is a massive one. 'The Debt of Honour Register' link offers an excellent search facility where the records of all victims can be consulted free of charge.

This is regularly used by a quarter-of-a-million people a week. There is also a telephone number for enquiries (01628 507200).

The 'What's New' link explains how the Commission still has ongoing battles to fight, to prevent cemeteries or important wartime locations being destroyed by road-building or similar types of development.

Meanwhile 'Education' explains the importance of helping the younger generation understand the magnitude of the sacrifice made on their behalf by their ancestors.

Following the 'Services' link well down the page, you will find links to the web pages of other organisations giving information about servicemen's records. Among them are links to commemorative organisations in Australia, New Zealand, Canada and Germany, to the National Ex-Prisoners of War Association, and to the Royal British Legion (see below).

www.britishlegion.org

The Royal British Legion is a well-known charitable organisation supporting ex-servicemen and their dependants. It does also have a commemorative function and, once you know where your relative(s) served, you will find the impressive list of onward links from this website extremely useful.

http://wargraves.freeyellow.com

War Graves in Britain takes a more personal approach. Kim Taylforth and John Oliver are interested in the more than 100,000 war graves in this country. Initially their interest was sparked by the one neglected grave of Private John Potts which turned into their passion. The website tells the story of all they have discovered about Private John Potts and his family.

www.army.mod.uk

The Ministry of Defence website is mainly concerned with the present day army but offers a search facility which may produce some helpful information about specific regiments. Contact details for the Army Records Office are given (records go from 1914 to 1992).

www.bbc.co.uk/history/lj/familylj/ gofurther_military.shtml

This will shortcut you to a page within the BBC's very extensive History website,

offering some useful World War links and a brief but relevant booklist.

www.fleetairarmarchive.net

The Fleet Air Arm Archive, 1939–1945, has a good website. Either scroll down the Index page or click on 'Roll of Honour' in the left-hand margin.

www.bbc.co.uk/history/war/ wwone/archives_02.shtml

The BBC History website has a six-page article by Peter Francis, 'Researching Military Records', that supplies some helpful guidance.

Lastly, don't ignore **'The National Roll of the Great War 1914–1918'**. This gives considerably more detail about the individual soldiers it lists than other sources.

You may have difficulty in finding the relevant volume, however, as even the Society of Genealogists only owns eight of the 14 volumes.

wills and probate records

Wills can vary from the most exciting source of family history details to total disappointment. The reading of them can be a significant challenge, mainly due to the use of archaic, often Latin phrases.

As you get into them, though, you will find that they tend to follow a pattern of terminology and use standard, frequently repetitious formulae. This will help you understand them much more rapidly.

By far the most difficult problem is locating them, since tracing their deposition is as complicated as anything in the family history search. Their storage tended to be based on religious divisions, so you may find yourself having to learn about Provinces, Dioceses, Prerogative Courts, Peculiars and Exempt Jurisdictions, among many other topics.

If you are researching in the earliest records, you should look out for a copy of Matthew's *Year Books of Probates 1630 to 1655*. Your subsequent research is best guided by a specialist book such as *Wills and their Whereabouts* by Anthony Camp. He also indexed the wills in the Prerogative Court of Canterbury between 1750 and 1800 (that took 6 volumes).

There are many other publications of indexes (for instance, by the British Record Society), but mostly you are referred to a specific library where you can obtain a photocopy of the will you are seeking.

For dating, remember that you are looking for a date of probate, not a date of writing or death, so any given will might be dated many years after the burial date.

If you have personal experience of wrestling with probate, you will probably notice that, by todays standards, probate was often granted in the past with admirable rapidity!

CD-roms include 'Index of Irish Wills 1484–1858' from Eneclann and 'Testamenta Vetusta: A collection of 803 Wills from the Twelfth to Sixteenth centuries' by Archive CD Books. See **www.archivecdbooks.com**.

www.courtservice.gov.uk/fandl/prob-guidance.htm
This Court Service website offers an admirably clear page headed Probate Records. It is a guide to obtaining copies of Probate Records, which is an ideal starting point for anyone approaching this topic.

www.gmcro.co.uk/wills.htm
The Greater Manchester County Record Office has a similarly clear page of explanations about Probate Records in England and Wales.

www.pro.gov.uk/research/leaflets/willsmain.htm
This page from the Family Records Centre is probably a useful next stage, presenting several links to leaflets explaining how to search the records. They suggest you print out these leaflets and bring them with you on a visit to the centre.

www.history.ac.uk/gh/probate.htm
The Guildhall Library's introduction to probate records in its possession is somewhat more detailed and more technical, though essential reading if you are serious about tracking down such material.

www.york.ac.uk/inst/bihr/probate%20.htm
The admirable Borthwick Institute in York, while clearly dealing with records local to Yorkshire, has good general information to offer relating to wills, as part of its family history web pages.

www.family-tree.co.uk
Family Tree Magazine has an excellent article, again by Anthony Camp, about Bank of England Will Extracts, in the May 2000 issue. The same author, a noted specialist in the field, contributed to another article on wills in the nineteenth century to the

December 2001 issue of the magazine. Details of this invaluable publication and its slightly more junior partner magazine, *Practical Family History*, are found here, though past articles are not, unfortunately, readable online.

www.genuki.org.uk/big/Gibson.html
See also this useful page about the Gibson Guides from GENUKI.

variant spellings

Before the second half of the nineteenth century spellings were very fluid. William Shakespeare's father John is listed with no fewer than 16 different variants of his name in the Council Book of Stratford Corporation.

The poet John Donne used variable spellings of the same words even within the same poem. Writing to his brother and sister-in-law in the US (yes, he had relatives who emigrated), John Keats used spellings that are either positively creative or very wayward – and this is at a date in the early years of the nineteenth century.

The other problem is that records, such as parish registers or county records, were often created as a result of dictation. When neither the bride nor groom, nor any of the witnesses to a marriage could sign their own names, it is hardly surprising if the vicar officiating on the day simply made a phonetic attempt at spelling the names he heard. As a result, the latter-day researcher is very much in the hands of an individual, how much education he had received, and how he felt on the day.

Early variants of spellings can be a problem, therefore, but can also be useful clues to pronunciation. The Rosier family of Rotherhithe had their name changed, for some unknown reason, to Rosher by a vicar in the 1790s. Earlier spellings include Rosyear, Roseare and Rossieare, which suggests that the 's' or 'ss' in the middle of the name was probably always pronounced 'sh'.

Similarly, James Brownhill was born in Timperley, Cheshire in 1832, but on 1 June 1856 he was married under the name Brownell, which only became clear when the entry was eventually found through his wife's name.

It is to be noted that he made his mark on his marriage certificate (he was a labourer, and couldn't write), so we can assume that he dropped the 'h' when pronouncing his name.

When searching any index of names before about 1850 (and indeed afterwards as well) it is vital to ensure you check all possible places where a relevant connection might be hiding. Some listings, such as the old microfiche version of the IGI, try to list similar sounding names in the same entry. Your own guesses at what alternative spellings are possible might be as good as theirs, so have the courage of your convictions and try those as well.

Many old indexes are ordered under first letters only, not alphabetically sifted within each letter thereafter. This means that in the wills index at the Family Records Centre, for example, you have to read all the Rs to find a Rosher entry in any particular year.

When using the Internet to search for names, and indeed for other things, such as vaguely remembered titles of books or elusive place names, do make use of the boolean search possibilities that many search engines allow.

The boolean search makes use of asterisks and similar symbols and can help you do what is sometimes called a fuzzy search. If you put the words 'boolean searching' into Google you will be offered several explanations. Make use of these and you are more likely to meet with success.

filling out the picture:
specialist sources

So far this book has been largely devoted to building up the family tree by tracing the vertical line from son to father. In other words, pursuing what we should strictly call genealogy.

Now we come to true family history, the business of filling out the picture laterally. For many researchers this is more fun, although identifying the relevant ancestors to investigate is obviously a necessary prerequisite. Some sort of genealogical line-building, however limited, has to come first.

The records you might investigate to help fill out the picture fall into two groups: those concerned with property and those concerned with people. Both can be informative, whether establishing where members of a family lived and how much property they owned, or what education they received and what profession they followed.

Any of these discoveries may lead into areas of further study. For example, you may find yourself exploring land tenure, with all its divisions and sub-divisions of agricultural land, measured in 'acres', 'roods' and 'poles'. Gradual acquisition of land can be an indicator of increasing wealth and, when its location is defined, of the development of particular farming or other interests.

House ownership can also be fascinating. The number of hearths or windows recorded for tax purposes is a useful gauge of prosperity since the majority of people had no more than one or two hearths. A householder who paid tax for half-a-dozen hearths was well off and almost certainly employed servants. Those taxed for 15 or 20 hearths were living in considerable style.

The records of persons, as opposed to property, are approximately listed in the order in which an individual might experience them. School, university and apprenticeship records come first, then records of trades or professions, followed by less general records, such as those for Workhouse occupants or criminals. This section ends with a major item on emigration and immigration, including the famous Ellis Island website in the US, and finally with obituaries.

This is a good moment to emphasise the importance of always making a note of your references. At the time of making a new discovery, it can seem very obvious where a particular record has been found, and you may not think it will be difficult to return to it at some later date.

However, it can be intensely frustrating to realise, some months or even years later, that you cannot remember where to look, and many fruitless hours will need to be spent searching.

So, if the mantra of the dedicated genealogist is 'check, check and check again', you should add to this the good practice of recording your sources every time.

poll books and electoral registers

Between 1696 and 1872 lists of voters in parliamentary elections, indicating which candidates(s) they had voted for, were frequently (though not annually) published in the form of Poll Books. These tended to be arranged by 'wapentakes' or by parishes and sometimes mentioned the addresses and occupations of voters. They do not exist for all counties and it is worth remembering that the right to vote was limited to those who owned land above a certain value, excluding not only women but also many tradesmen.

The Reform Act of 1832 and subsequent Acts in the nineteenth and early twentieth centuries extended the right to vote gradually. It was not until 1928, with the Representation of the People Act, that women over the age of 21 were finally enfranchised. The age was lowered in 1969 to 18 for both men and women. Electoral registers can help suggest dates of birth, if you know what the voting age was at the given period. By comparison with today, a far higher proportion of those eligible to vote tended to do so.

www.soft.net.uk/samjraymond/pb2.html
A very useful facsimile series is in the process of being brought out by S.A. & M.J. Raymond of Exeter. They have already re-published 15 Poll Books, covering different counties and dates, and others are to follow. This web page gives a list and contact details, and you can order by email. The cost of facsimile reproduction is high, so these books retail at between £15.00 and £25.00.

www.bl.uk/collections/wider/ genealogyref.html#POLL
A small feature about poll books and electoral registers is offered here by the British Library, with links to relevant offerings from the Institute of Historical Research (**www. history.ac.uk**) and the Guildhall Library (**www.history.ac._uk/gh**), the principal

depositories of poll books. The British Library has copies of most electoral registers.

Among the excellent series of Gibson Guides is the title *Poll Books c. 1696–1872* by Jeremy Gibson and Colin Rogers, published in 1994 by the Federation of Family History Societies. This helps to find what poll books exist and where they may be consulted.

County Record Offices and Libraries hold copies of relevant local poll books. Researchers will find other volumes in antiquarian book dealers' catalogues, which are worth snapping up if you have identified a location and date. They may be expensive.

tithe redemption maps and surveys

Tithe maps, as they are commonly called, were created as a result of the Tithe Commutation Act of 1836. This Act was passed to address the problem for clergy, who received part of their stipend as tithes (the word 'tithe' means one tenth of the value of the produce from an individual's land) from the properties in the parish – which they had difficulty in claiming.

The maps were the result of surveys carried out by specially appointed Tithe Commissioners between 1336 and 1854 to determine the proper valuation of the tithes, and allow them to be bought out. The maps are accompanied by details of tithe apportionment, which describes the plot, its owner, its tenant, the current purpose (crops, pasture etc.) and the value.

Tithe maps cover about 79 per cent of England and Wales at a scale varying between 26 and 13 inches to the mile. They contain enormous detail, including the identification of individual houses – they were the first large-scale 'national survey'. Care must be taken, as they are not always accurate, and some disappointments are inevitable when you find that the map you want doesn't exist or has got lost. However, in general they are an informative and helpful resource. They are kept in County Record Offices and the PRO at Kew.

That mainstay of *Family History Magazine*, John Titford, contributed a helpful and approbatory review of the book *Tithe Surveys for Historians* by Roger J.P. Kain and Hugh C. Prince, published by Phillimore & Co., in the Novmber 2000 edition.

http://catalogue.pro.gov.uk/Leaflets/ri2148.htm
The Public Records Office offers the feature 'Tithe Maps: A Detailed Examination'. Worth reading as an introduction to the topic.

www.westminster.gov.uk/libraries/archives/guide/guide07.cfm
www.westminster.gov.uk/libraries/archives/guide/guide23.cfm
The PRO also offers these two pages, 'Tithe Files, Maps and Apportionments' and 'Parish Summaries'. Further related material is accessible from the 'next' button at the bottom of the page. Large illustrations make loading slower than usual.

http://catalogue.pro.gov.uk/Leaflets/ri2177.htm
Staying with the PRO, here is an explanation of the introduction of the Ordnance Survey in 1791.

www.westminster.gov.uk/libraries/archives/guide/guide07.cfm
Westminster City Council introduces its four-and-a-half thousand maps that form their fine collection on the cartographical history of London.

www.ex.ac.uk/geography/research/maphist.html
Exeter University is noted for its studies in the history of cartography, which it introduces here with a link to a specialist feature on tithe maps. It also mentions several books worth consulting.

www.llgc.org.uk/dm/dm0030.htm
The National Library of Wales looks at the history and availability of tithe maps in detail.

http://proni.nics.gov.uk/records/tithe.htm
PRONI covers Northern Ireland but is slightly less detailed than the site above.

www.jams.swinternet.co.uk/Maps.htm
Jean Manco's personal page simply headed 'Maps' introduces some good onward links.

www.hmc.gov.uk/focus/your_history/housesources.htm
For those researching the history of a house this is a useful page.

pipe rolls and manorial records

By the time you become interested in pipe rolls or manorial records, you will have already gone a long way back in your research and will be beginning to fill out the background. You will need to have acquired considerable skills in reading medieval Latin and old handwriting (see pages 145–46 and 150–153 for assistance).

Pipe rolls are nothing more than the description of the way old records were stored. The writing was on a long single sheet of parchment, sometimes over 20-ft long. This then had to be kept, so it was rolled up and stored in a pipe to protect it. Pipes could be stacked up in the archive, while still allowing lower rolls to be withdrawn.

The information the pipe rolls contain could be anything that was recorded at the time. So, for those of a truly 'researching' and persistent nature they may prove an invaluable stepping stone.

Because of their antiquity you are only likely to meet them in places such as the Public Record Office or other major record offices.

Manorial records are the records of a particular manor. A medieval manor was one of the smaller units of the feudal land hierarchy. It was held in fief by a 'Lord of the Manor', who was emphatically not noble. Before the Conquest there were about 4,000 manorial lordships. A manor can itself be divided into submanors; Hemel Hempstead is divided into at least seven, the two largest of which are now separate parishes: Bovingdon and Flauden.

There is a lively commercial market in Lordships of the Manor, and prices can be very high, as many overseas contenders, particularly American, will be bidding (see the feature on the Nobility, pages 116–17).

For further information the first place to look is the Manorial Society of Great Britain on 020 7735 6633. The Historical Manuscripts Commission maintains the Manorial Documents Register and the National Register of Archives, which lists the whereabouts of such material.

www.medievalgenealogy.org.uk/guide/man.shtml
Notes on Medieval English Genealogy comes up with a good feature, this time on 'Manorial Documents.' The explanation of what manorial records contain is followed by an impressive number of links. Many scanned documents are readable online, though are not necessarily presented in their entirety. A similarly good page on pipe rolls within the same website is available at: **www.medievalgenealogy.org.uk/guide/pip.shtml**.

http://catalogue.pro.gov.uk/Leaflets/ri2219.htm
Manorial Records in the Public Record Office is a drier account – but is detailed and reliable – with a link to an associated page, Manor and other Local Court Rolls. Other links go to the PRO's own collections. For Pipe Rolls see **http://catalogue.pro.gov.uk/Leaflets/ri2138.htm** and **www.pro.gov.uk/virtualmuseum/millennium/piperoll/piperoll/default.htm**, a feature

from the PRO's Virtual Museum describing and illustrating the first pipe roll.

www.sog.org.uk/acatalog/SoG_Bookshop
_Online_Manorial_Records_64.html
The Society of Genealogists lists the publications available from its online bookshop relating to manorial records. They range from a 22-page booklet, 'How to locate and use manorial records' by P. Palgrave Moore, costing £1.75, to the 750-page *Medieval Society and the Manor Court* edited by Zvi Razi and Richard Smith, costing £75.00.

www.hmc.gov.uk/mdr/bibliog.htm
The Historical Manuscripts Commission provides a very considerable reading list of titles relevant to the use of manorial records.

www.genfair.com/greenpages/leases.htm
Genfair's page on 'Manorial Leases for Genealogists' should convince you of the importance of overcoming the difficulty of reading manorial records.

hearth tax, window tax and land tax

hearth tax

Hearth Tax, or 'chimney money' as it was called, was introduced in 1662. It was withdrawn in 1689, so was only levied for 27 years. Crown revenues of £1.2-million were needed annually, but Customs, Excise and other duties fell short by about £170,000.

With the rate of tax being set at two shillings per annum per hearth, or fireplace, it was hoped that Hearth Tax would raise this sum – only about £115,000 was raised (1662–1664). Part of the reason was inefficient collection. Hearth Tax was collected twice a year, on Lady Day (25 March) and Michaelmas (29 September), by the sheriff or his nominated deputies. People in poverty could be granted a discharge certificate, though their names were still listed in the roll.

These rolls survive to a varying degree. Wiltshire has a roll survival rate of less than a third, while Nottingham is very complete for 1664 and 1674. The rolls are published in a variety of formats by different publishers. They are useful if you are fortunate enough to be researching an unusual surname, when one can pick up residence in a village, together with an idea of the scale of the property. Also, because ordinary people are named, including people possessing no more than a single hearth, the list is cut deep socially. No information other than the number of hearths, however, is recorded.

http://catalogue.pro.gov.uk/Leaflets/ri2139.htm
The Public Record Office gives one of the clearest explanations of Hearth Tax and its uses.

www.pro.gov.uk/virtualmuseum/millennium/piperoll/tax/default.htm
The PRO's 'virtual museum' displays a hearth tax return from Pudding Lane, where the hearth that notoriously started the Great Fire of London in 1666 was located. A link from this page leads to more generalised information.

window tax

Window Tax was introduced in 1696 as a replacement for Hearth Tax. It was brought in during the reign of William of Orange to pay for the minting of new coinage. Window Tax lasted much longer than its predecessor, only being repealed in 1851 when it was combined with House Tax.

In 1696 all houses were charged at two shillings, while properties with 10 to 20 windows paid four shillings, and those with more than 20 windows paid eight shillings. By 1747 the charges had been scaled in a more sophisticated way to penalise the most prosperous homes. At this date we find houses with 15 to 19 windows being charged at nine pence per window and those with 20 or more windows at one shilling per window.

The charges were sufficiently punitive for many house-owners to block up windows that were not essential. Owners who wished to impress others sometimes faced their homes with more windows than actually functioned, even though they actually paid tax for fewer windows than were outwardly seen. It may be the case that the term 'daylight robbery' originated from Window Tax which, in causing the poor to brick up some windows, made homes much darker.

http://dspace.dial.pipex.com/town/ terrace/adw03/c-eight/taxpitt.htm

From this Web of English History website there is a useful page here on Pitt the Younger's political and economic reasons for increasing the already much-hated window tax.

land tax

Land Tax was introduced in 1692 and technically remained in force until 1961. The assessment was organised by 'hundreds' or 'wapentakes' (sub-divisions of counties), and then by parishes and villages. Land Tax records were also used as a means of establishing who was entitled to vote.

These records tend to be found in County Record Offices, but their survival is patchy. Some duplicate records may be found in Quarter Session Records. Almost the entire return for one particular year, 1798, is held at the PRO (class IR.23).

In theory the full return contains: the names of proprietors and copyholders (be warned that the word 'late' before a name may indicate either a recent death or merely that the persons concerned had moved); the name of the occupier; the name or description of the property (this is not generally recorded before 1825/6); the sums assessed and 'exonerated' and the amount of tax levied. In some cases (like Little Sutton in Cheshire), all the researcher will find is a pile of slips with names of occupiers and values of assessment for the village.

A useful book is *Land and Window Tax Assessments* by Jeremy Gibson, Mervyn Medlycott & Dennis Mills, published in 1998.

www.history.ac.uk/gh/landtax.htm
This Guildhall Library page is entitled 'Land Tax Assessments for The City of London'.

http://members.lycos.co.uk/bookhistory/taxbgn.html
The London Book Trades Project addresses the question of land tax from a different viewpoint but is useful in explanatory terms.

www.nas.gov.uk/miniframe/fact_sheet/valuationrolls.pdf
The National Archives of Scotland provide a page of information and some links relating to land tax.

www.ex.ac.uk/~RDavies/arian/current/howmuch.html
This web page from Roy Davies' extensive historical website, looks at how we can assess the current value of old money. With some warnings about how to interpret the tables, it leads to other useful sources of financial information.

www.pickeringchatto.com/taxation.htm
For those who want to explore the subject in exhaustive detail, Pickering Chatto offer this eight-volume work, edited by D.P. O'Brien, *The History of Taxation*. If you scroll down, the publishers' 'blurb' is informative.

www.inlandrevenue.gov.uk/history/taxhiso.htm
If you are wondering when Income Tax came in, here is the answer: it was introduced by William Pitt the Younger to fund the Napoleonic Wars in 1799, even though in the previous year he stated that the obligation to reveal one's personal wealth for tax purposes 'was repugnant to the customs and manners of the nation'. This page is the introduction to a series of further pages, telling the story of Income Tax from then until now, in most interesting and entertaining detail.

rates and valuation office records

The earliest rate books date from the eighteenth century and often give helpful details about both the householder and the premises. The Valuation Office, founded in 1909, also assessed property for tax purposes. Valuation Books and Field Books, of which not all survive, can be found in County Record Offices or the Public Record Office.

school and university records

Education was a privilege rather than a right until 1870, when it was first made available for children up to the age of 10. Even then it was not compulsory until a decade later. Your chances of tracing the school record of an ancestor before then aren't good. The records of schools and universities, however, can be fruitful areas for research. In some cases they are very substantial.

Among the best are those of the universities of Oxford and Cambridge, given that for many centuries all well-educated young men attended one or the other. Copies of *Alumni Oxoniensis 1500–1886* by Foster (1891) and *Alumni Cantabrigiensis from the Earliest Times to 1900* by Venn and Venn (1922) contain a fabulous amount of information dating back to the sixteenth century.

The latter can now be searched online via Ancestry.com (see **www.ancestry.com/ search/rectype/directories/cambridge/ main.htm**). They tend to show the student's age at entry and the degrees obtained, as well as the father's name and place of residence. They may also show the school(s) previously attended and give some information on the student's career.

Many other universities have similar records. For instance, there is a *Roll of Graduates of the University of Glasgow 1727–1897* by W. Innes Addison; or *Alumni Dubliniensis 1593–1846* by Burtchall and

Sadleir. Schools also publish lists of past pupils, which means that some have pupil lists covering several hundred years. The schools may still possess these records; otherwise try the Local Educational Authority and the County Record Office.

It was a common practice to give books as prizes to children who performed well. These are quite often well cared for and handed down in families. They usually display a bookplate or some other identification and details of the achievement for which it was presented.

As you seek to track down the records of schools, remember that some schools have been re-named. If you appear to be drawing a blank it is worth enquiring at the Local Educational Authority about any past changes of name.

Colin Chapman is an expert in the field of education records and has published the following two books, which should be of use to anyone starting to explore this area of research: *Using Education Records* and *The Growth of British Education and its Records* published by Lochin Publishing.

There is no better description to describe these books than the publisher's own: 'An historical description of education and the present whereabouts of its records in England, Wales, Scotland and Ireland. Schools of every description, universities, reformatories, military and adult academies were provided by the State, by charities, by endowments, by religious bodies of all denominations, by professional institutions and by individuals. Of great help to family, social and educational historians are the surviving records of student admissions and attendances, teachers' log books, reports, honours and awards, punishments, accounts and managers' and governors' meetings. This indexed book identifies where these records may be found with numerous addresses to contact given throughout the text.'

**www.bishopdale.demon.co.uk/fhs/
index.html**

From the website of the Upper Dales Family History Group (in this instance the Yorkshire Dales), select the link to Angela Petyt's 'The History and Records of Education'. This gives an admirably clear list of the various types of education establishment and the records that may survive.

For those researching in Northern Ireland, The Public Record Office of Northern Ireland (PRONI) has released a 'Guide to Educational Records'.

apprentice and guild records

The system of apprenticing young people, often children as young as 12, dates from medieval times. Boys, and some girls, went to work for an employer to learn a particular craft or trade. The child's parents paid for this training, which would typically last between seven and 10 years. Fees could be considerable, from £20 to £100 during the reign of James I, for example. An apprenticeship normally ended at the age of 21 or when the young person got married. In 1563, the regulations governing apprenticeship were formalised under the Statute of Apprentices, which obliged all prospective tradesmen to serve an apprenticeship first, that was taught by a guild member.

Pauper children, known as 'Poor Law' apprentices, were often apprenticed at an even younger age, as a means of getting them into employment and consequently no longer dependent on the charity of the parish. On completion of an apprenticeship, the young man became known as a 'journeyman', which meant he could begin earning for the first time. He would now start saving money to set up in trade on his own.

Craftsmen in the same trade formed the first guilds in London during the reign of Henry II, and membership of a guild acted as a guarantee of a certain standard of work. Shoddy work or over-pricing was policed by the guild and those guilty of such practices were fined and obliged to do the work again.

Expulsion from the guild was the ultimate sanction. This very severe punishment meant that the man concerned could no longer ply his trade in the same town. In times of hardship or ill-health, however, the guild would support its members and their dependants. The Guilds were the first trade unions, quite literally, in that they were created to protect and promote the skills and artisans of a particular trade.

http://catalogue.pro.gov.uk/Leaflets/ri2187.htm

The PRO comes up with the clearest explanation of the apprenticeship system. The same article can be accessed from GENUKI. Apprentice records can be seen in Apprentices of Great Britain (indexed to 1774) at the PRO.

www.cityoflondon.gov.uk/leisure_heritage /libraries_archives_museums_galleries/ assets/pdf/pb_apprentices.pdf

This page explains apprenticeship record holdings in the Guildhall Library and makes the important point that many arrangements for apprenticeship were completely informal. Therefore, it could be the case that there are no surviving records.

http://freespace.virgin.net/owston.tj/ apprent.htm

Timothy Owston's personal website contains this page explaining the difference between trade apprentices and poor apprentices.

www.englishorigins.com/lonapps-details.html

English Origins in association with the Society of Genealogists has this useful page giving details of London Apprenticeship Abstracts 1531–1850.

**www.nas.gov.uk/miniframe/fact_sheet/
crafts.pdf**

The National Archives of Scotland present a page on Guild Records as held by them.

www.history.ac.uk/gh/livdet.html

The Guildhall Library Manuscripts Section lists among its Leaflet Guides To Records: Sources for Tracing Apprenticeship and Membership in City Livery Companies and Related Organisations.

**www.englishorigins.com/liverycompanies.
html**

The useful English Origins website, which is associated with the Society of Genealogists, has details here of the London Livery Companies. There is some good explanatory material and a complete list of the various trades covered, with a good number of these offering links to further information, usually to the websites of the individual guilds themselves, in cases where these still exist.

**www.ancientquest.com/embark/
guilds.shtml**

Ancient Quest Seminars has this excellent article on Medieval Guilds, helpfully explaining the difference between merchant guilds and craft guilds.

**www.wealddown.co.uk/worshipful-
company-of-plumbers-detail.htm**

For a good explanation of the origins and practice of a single guild, in this case the plumbers, this page from the Weald and Downland Museum's website is informative.

trade and county directories

Directories were first produced in London in the seventeenth century (the earliest, dating from 1677, claims to be 'the oldest printed list of the merchants and bankers of London'). During the next 100 years they became increasingly widespread and useful.

By 1793 *The Universal British Directory* was appearing, covering most large towns in the country. Soon afterwards Ireland was covered (Holden's 1805 *Triennial Directory of 85 Irish Towns*). By the nineteenth century many different publishers were at work, including Pigot, Kelly, Slater, White and the Post Office.

These directories usually covered businesses, and sometimes private addresses, which means that you may learn what your ancestors did, where they worked and where they lived. They often include sections on 'gentry', schools, public houses, the professions and farmers. You stand a reasonable chance of finding your own ancestors if they lived in a town.

It is often the case that, if you can identify one ancestor in a particular trade, you will find others, as patrimony (or nepotism if one is being critical) was very often the route by which people were admitted to particular trades.

Although the bulk of any of these publications will be simply a list of names, professions and residences, they also usually offer a certain amount of peripheral detail and supplementary material. *The Universal British Directory,* for example, lists not only the inhabitants of London (and in other volumes all other major towns and villages in England and Wales), it also lists members of both Houses of Parliament, the navy, the army, departments of state and public offices, the Post Office, magistrates, bankers etc. Pigot's *A Directory of London and its Suburbs* covers public transport, markets, owners of bathhouses, newspapers etc. and ends with a selection of advertisements.

Many of these books are not indexed. Early indexes tended to be arranged by initial letter and thereafter the order was often haphazard. A read-through of such directories is the only way of checking the information contained. Few volumes are long and the social and commercial detail they provide is often fascinating in itself.

A specialist bookseller of early directories is Ray Sparkes (Books) of Yoxall, Staffordshire (01543 472274) for printed originals; and Archive CD Books at **www.archivecdbooks. com** publish facsimile versions on CD (viewed through Acrobat). Similar lists of directories on CD are available from Back to Roots at **www.backtoroots.co.uk/ page2.htm** and from Stepping Stones at **www.stepping-stones.co.uk/htdocs/ trade.cfm.**

www.genuki.org.uk/indexes/ENGcontents. html

'English Trade Directories of the Nineteenth Century' is a page within GENUKI supplied by Sue O'Neill who gives a good explanation of what such directories contain. There are some onward links to Pigot's for Berkshire, Buckinghamshire, Wiltshire and Worcestershire (these can be read online).

www.genuki.org.uk/big/eng

This is the invaluable starting point for locating trade directories (and a great deal more besides) nationwide. For example, select 'Durham' as the county you wish to investigate, scroll down to the list of resources and select 'Trade Directories'. You will be taken to a page offering, in this instance, two further links: 'Trade Directory Holdings in Northern Libraries' and directories available on microfiche from 'North Fiche'. Clicking on these will give further details, telling you where such material can be consulted.

www.direct-resources.uk.com/ surname.htm

Direct Resources 'presents 474,236 surnames from the 40 English counties in or around 1848'. This is a most useful facility, offering names and towns either in text or Excel file form, and readable online free of charge. The advantage of the Excel files, is that you can re-sort the names alphabetically, which is very helpful. To do this, select **all the data** on a given page, go to 'data' in the top toolbar, and then to 'sort' and select 'Column A ascending'. This will re-shuffle the information correctly, whereas selecting the surname column alone will not. Excel provides a warning to help you avoid this easily-made mistake.

www.sog.org.uk/acatalog/SoG_Bookshop_Online_Counties_of_England-140.html

The Society of Genealogists' Bookshop can supply many trade directories and similar publications on CD-rom. Starting from this page, select the relevant county and follow the prompts. When you have identified the CD you want, you can buy it online in the normal way by adding it to the 'shopping cart'.

www.cityoflondon.gov.uk/leisure_heritage/libraries_archives_museums_galleries/assets/pdf/pb_directories.pdf

The Guildhall Library's web page addresses may seem excessively long, but using them will often prove a far quicker route to the specific page than going in through the main URL and trying to access the same information from the homepage. This one is headed 'Trade Directories and Telephone Books at Guildhall Library' and gives a clear account of what the Library possesses, as well as suggested further reading.

www.archivebritain.com/genealogical_resources.htm

Archive Britain publishes historical material on CD-rom. If you scroll down the page you will find the link to Street, Residential, Commercial and Trade Directories.

www.thegenealogist.co.uk/cddata.htm

The Genealogist lists 'UK Genealogy Data CDs and Discs', covering a huge range of topics, including trade and county directories.

www.royalwarrant.org/Association.asp

The Royal Warrant Holders' Association has its website here, with an interesting small feature on its history and the pride its members take in supplying goods and services to the Crown.

www.bodley.ox.ac.uk/johnson/exhibition
The John Johnson Collection Exhibition 2001: the Ephemera of Trade is the online-readable catalogue of an exhibition shown at the Bodleian Library in Oxford. If you have a little time to spend, click into contents in the left-hand index and explore the history of trade ephemera from 1654 to the 1860s, such as trade cards, shop signs and the like. The numerous illustrations load quickly and the accompanying notes are completely fascinating.

military and naval history

army lists and militia assessments

Prior to there being any form of regular army, small fighting forces had been mustered at times of national danger by those who owed a duty of service to the King, in approximate proportion to their status. There was, however, no regular army as we understand it today. Even during the Civil War, the King's forces (the Cavaliers) still fought in a somewhat medieval style, whereas those commanding Cromwell's New Model Army (the Roundheads or Parliamentarians) – formed in 1645 under Sir Thomas Fairfax – operated in a more 'drilled' or disciplined manner.

The regular standing army was formed by the 'restored' King, Charles II, on 7 January 1661, following the Civil War. From that date onwards, the regimental structure of the army was based on the areas from which men volunteered, and lists of officers were published. For instance, the 22nd Regiment of Foot was formed in Chester in 1689 on the accession to the throne of William and Mary, when men were invited to enrol in support of the King against the threat of James II. Five other regiments were formed in that year and four the previous year. This information is available in the Army Lists.

The first true Army List was brought out by Nathan Brooks in 1612, detailing the officers in the army of that date. The list of officers in the Roundhead and Cavalier armies of 1642 was published by Edward Peacock in 1863. The period from 1661 to 1714 was covered by Charles Dalton in six volumes, entitled *English Army Lists and Commission Registers*, published in 1960. It was not until 1740, however, that the Secretary of State for War gave permission for an official Army List. Copies of that list, and all subsequent lists published annually, can be found in the PRO at Kew, the SoG library, and some other major libraries.

Militia Assessments were the consequence of the Militia Acts of 1662 and 1663, which were enacted for the defence of the realm in the period before the standing army became fully effective. In 1803, there was a new requirement for national defence to meet the threat from Napoleon. The assessments were carried out by county, and several have been published.

Their real advantage as compared with the Army Lists is that they name ordinary 'soldiers', not just officers, and so are far more useful. Individuals tended to be recorded by parish in a county, and in some cases the record will list a peace-time profession. The original documents, where they have survived, will probably be found in county record offices.

The best documented army records date from the First World War onwards, and details of how to search these are given on pages 53–55.

To find earlier records check out **The Public Record Office** at Kew and the **Family Records Centre** in Myddelton Street which are the two major depositories for all documents relating to service personnel. Generally the early records are held at the PRO and the more recent ones (Boer War as well as the two World Wars) at the FRC. More than half the early military records were, however, lost in a bombing raid during World War II.

If you put words such as 'armies medieval' into the Google search engine to find information about the history of British warfare, you will actually be presented with a multiplicity of websites concerned with wargaming, model miniatures, book offers and battle re-enactments. Ignoring these, however, the following will give you some helpful background information:

www.genuki.org.uk/big/Military Records.html

GENUKI provides this most important source for Army, Navy and Air Force records, offering a huge list of links, which you will be able to spend many happy (and fruitful) hours exploring.

www.sog.org.uk/acatalog/SoG_Bookshop _Online_General_Titles_255.html

The Society of Genealogists lists disks, books and booklets available from its bookshop, all concerned with military and naval records. These can all be ordered online.

www.phancocks.pwp.blueyonder.co.uk/ localhistory/mid-age.htm

Here there is a useful article entitled 'The Middle Ages – The Beauchamp Period' which, although focusing on local detail about two villages in Worcestershire, paints a picture that would have been widely applicable at that time.

www.pillagoda.freewire.co.uk/CRECY.htm

'Winter's Bloom' is a fascinating single page describing the forces that took part in the Battle of Crecy in 1346.

http://web.ukonline.co.uk/glenn.foard/ english_civil_war.htm

Glenn Foard's English Civil War pages, within his English Battles and Sieges website, are very interesting and detailed.

www.bbc.co.uk/history/war/ englishcivilwar/west_01.shtml

An article entitled 'The Civil War in the West', by Dr John Wroughton, is presented under the BBC History umbrella. It loads pages singly, so you have the slightly irritating necessity of clicking the 'next' button, but it is informative and well written.

www.pro.gov.uk/pathways/FamilyHistory/gallery3/britarmy.htm

The Public Record Office's page entitled 'The British Army before the First World War' introduces the topic clearly and offers onward links leading to more detailed information about the PRO's military holdings.

www.nas.gov.uk/miniframe/fact_sheet/military.pdf

The National Archives of Scotland's military records are introduced here.

http://dspace.dial.pipex.com/forrestdale/ArmyLists.html

Forrest Anderson has a good introduction to the topic of Army Lists here, within his Forrestdale Research website (though his offer of doing research is temporarily suspended due to other work commitments).

navy records

Many of the websites already listed above will cover Naval as well as Army records. The following, however, are more navy-specific:

www.nmm.ac.uk

The National Maritime Museum's website, though much improved from a couple of years ago, is still not the most easily navigable. The two links at the very bottom of the homepage, 'Centre for Research' and 'Manuscripts Catalogue' will be most useful for the family historian.

www.mariners-l.freeserve.co.uk/UKPages.htm#preRN

Mariners is a portal website for a number of other navy-related sites and pages. It is rich in interesting information. Coastguards' records are also available from this website.

www.royalnavalmuseum.org

The Royal Naval Museum at Portsmouth is another major source of naval information (and interest) but is not a depository for naval records. 'Permanent Collections' is the first link to try, and then 'Manuscript Collection' from that page. Otherwise try both 'Library' and 'Publications'.

www.chris.watts.ukgateway.net/merchsea. htm#chap4
Merchant Seamen of Britain and its Former Colonies is a website run by brothers, Christopher T. and Michael J. Watts, regular contributors to *Family History Magazine*. This page gives extensive details of their book *My Ancestor was a Merchant Seaman*, whose second edition will be the definitive text for those seeking information about ancestors in the Merchant Navy.

www.simonides.org/links/research/ research.html
This webpage, simply headed Research Sites, offers another very extensive list of links to sites of military and naval interest, past and present, British and worldwide.

records of clergymen

Crockford's *Clerical Directory* lists the names of Church of England clergy and parishes in the UK, along with those in the Church of Wales and the Episcopal Church of Scotland. It has been published most years since 1858, though now it only appears every three years or so. Past copies are often available in libraries, and will usually provide an individual's date and location of ordination and current address. Further information such as education and past benefices held may also be given. Using this as a guide to relevant parish(es), you can sometimes look up such details as the population of each parish and the stipend it paid.

Prior to 1858, other publications, such as the *Clerical Guide* (first published 1817) and the *Clergy List* (first published 1841) give some assistance, though they are by no means as comprehensive as Crockford's.

In addition, the names of many Church of England clergy are given in Joseph Foster's *Index Ecclesiasticus 1800–1840*. If you are researching earlier you will need diocesan records of ordination and presentations.

The equivalent to Crockford's for Roman Catholic Clergy is *The Catholic Directory* published annually since 1851, though earlier, less complete editions do exist. Another major source of information is the publication *Catholic Missions and Registers 1700–1880*, a major work in six volumes by Michael Gandy.

If you are lucky enough to find a vicar in the family tree, remember that he will almost certainly have been to university, which means that prior to about 1850 he was probably educated at Oxford or Cambridge (see page 71). Incidentally, remember that diocesan boundaries have not always been geographically fixed, so you may need to look in adjacent areas to find the parish or parishes in which you have connections.

Family Tree Magazine, Volume 17, No. 3 (January 2001) has an excellent article by Anthony Camp entitled 'Clergymen of the Church of England'. It also points out other sources, such as the *Gentleman's Magazine* and the records of charitable organisations.

For general purposes start with the GENUKI website (see page 29), which has records of both Church of England and Non-Conformist clergymen. The Family Records Centre is a major holder of such records, though the collections of local county libraries should also be consulted.

www.lambethpalacelibrary.org/holdings/ Guides/clergyman.html
Research Guides: Biographical Sources for Anglican Clergy. This is a page introducing the records held by Lambeth Palace Library. Among them are the Caution Books 1758–1884 which gave warnings to Bishops about inadequate clergymen in their dioceses.

www.personal.rdg.ac.uk/~lhstalrs/cced.htm

The Clergy of the Church of England Database is a project planned to run for five years, from October 1999. It aims to database Church of England clergymen between 1540 and 1835. Further information about this project is available from **www.kcl.ac.uk/humanities/cch/cce/about.htm**.

www.history.qmul.ac.uk/staff/Clergy.htm

This single page introduces both the book and CD-rom, *Clergy in London in the Late Middle Ages*, by Virginia Davis, providing the ordination details of more than 30,000 records of secular and regular clergy from 1361 to 1539, including some members of religious orders.

www.history.ac.uk/gh/clergy.htm

This page introduces the Guildhall Library Manuscripts Section 'Sources For Tracing Clergy and Lay Persons'.

http://rylibweb.man.ac.uk/data1/dg/methodist/methguid.html

The Methodist Archives and Research Centre is run by the excellent John Rylands Library at Manchester University.

www.leeds.ac.uk/library/spcoll/quaker/quakint1.htm

The Quaker Archives database is held by Leeds University.

www.re-serve.co.uk/wrlinks.htm

For a major set of multi-faith links that may in some cases lead to other sources of historical information, try this very useful list.

records of lawyers and the law

The law has always given a good living to a bright young man. A brief look at Trade Directories reveals how many lawyers were practising in even the smaller towns.

From early times the profession has been divided into barristers and solicitors (called attorneys until 1875). Among the Inns of Court in London, where barristers became members, were the Inner and Middle Temples and Lincoln's and Gray's Inns. These still survive today, though others like Clifford's Inn, Clement's Inn or Thavie's Inn have disappeared. The 'Bench' books are a source of lists of names, so called because members of the Inns were known as 'benchers'. These books should be sought in libraries.

Judges were chosen from barristers. See Edward Foss's *Biographical Dictionary of the Judges of England 1066–1870* (published 1870). Judges also appear in the *Dictionary of National Biography*.

Anthony Camp's excellent article in the March 2001 issue of *Family History Magazine*, 'Records of Lawyers in England and Wales', goes into far greater detail than can be addressed here, covering Justices of the Peace and Civil or Canon Lawyers as well as solicitors, barristers and judges.

The Law List 1812 is available on microfiche from the Society of Genealogists. See **www.sog.org.uk/acatalog/SoG_Bookshop _Online_Law__Chancery_176.html** for this and other relevant publications (in book form) from the SoG Bookshop.

In general, histories of the legal profession in any online form appear scarce, but there are several valuable books on the topic:

Lawyers, Litigation and English Society since 1450 by Christopher Brooks looks at legal procedure in England over the centuries and the changes in the education of members of the legal profession.

Law and Authority in Early Modern England 1485–1660 by the same author is in preparation; and he is currently working on the period 1625–1688 for the Oxford History of the Laws of England, a multi-volume publication that will in due course replace Sir William Holdsworth's classic *A History of English Law*.

The Common Law Tradition: Lawyers, Books and the Law by J.H. Baker studies the Inns of Court and Chancery as well as the work of local courts. It looks at the traditions that have evolved as part of the legal profession in general, including its education, use of language, court conventions and presentation.

The Making of the Common Law and *The Origins of the English Legal Profession*, both by Paul Brand, do more than simply look at legal doctrine. They study those who have shaped English law over the centuries, and specific cases that have influenced legal practice today.

English Criminal Justice in the Nineteenth Century by David Bentley shows how attitudes to crime and punishment have changed enormously since Victorian times and explores why those changes came about, whether as a result of pressure from outside or from within the legal profession.

www.online-law.co.uk/bar/lincolns/history

'An Introduction to Lincoln's Inn' is presented here by Sir Robert Megarry, one of a series of articles available from this Online Law website. Click the 'Origins' link to explore further.

www.venables.co.uk/barinns.htm

'Inns of Court' links maintained by Delia Venables is a shortcut to the websites of the four currently existing Inns of Court.

www.frankcass.com/jnls/jlh.htm

'The Journal of Legal History', published by Frank Cass Publishers, is a serious academic periodical that will mainly interest specialists but it may be worth scrolling through the lists of recent articles to see if there is anything of relevance to your personal researches.

medical records

The early medical profession was not the specialist trade that it is today. The first practitioners were monastic, and most monasteries had a herb garden. Later doctors often combined the job with that of hairdresser, as barber-surgeons. Surgeons prescribed physic (medicine) and apothecaries (precursors of pharmacists) also practised.

Lists occur for some areas, for example 'The Medical Profession in Hull 1400–1900' by J. and M. Bickford and 'The Medical Practitioners of Medieval England, A Biographical Register' by Talbot and Hammond. Jan Bondeson's book, *A Cabinet of Medical Curiosities*, is a fascinating look at the conflict between medicine and science from a historical perspective.

A good starting point for seeking out health records is 'Sources for Medical Men' by Anthony Camp in the February 2001 issue of *Family Tree Magazine*.

The Royal College of Physicians, set up in 1518, has published *The Royal College of Physicians and its Collections: An Illustrated History*. Details of this book, with some sample pages, can be viewed at **www.rcplondon.ac.uk/pubs/books/ih/index.htm**, and the book can be ordered.

The famous Munk's Rolls, as they are known, are biographies of Royal College physicians, in seven volumes by W. Munk (vols. 1–3, 1518–1825 include licenciates; vols. 4–7, 1826–1983, list fellows only).

The Royal College of Surgeons tells its own history online at **www.rcseng.ac.uk/welcome/history_of_the_college** but deflects genealogical enquiries to any of the following: The Guildhall Library, London Metropolitan Archives, The Public Record Office, The Society of Genealogists, UK Family History Online, GENUKI or the Wellcome Library for the History and Understanding of Medicine (see next page).

www.wellcome.ac.uk
The Wellcome Trust is a charity whose mission is 'to foster and promote research with the aim of improving human and animal health'. From its index select 'Library' to find the Wellcome Library for the History and Understanding of Medicine, explaining the historical material the Trust possesses. Another page, **www.wellcome.ac.uk/en/library/homlib/sources/src10.html**, has links to military hospitals and overseas hospitals as well as those in Britain.

http://hospitalrecords.pro.gov.uk
The Hospital Records Database is a joint project between the PRO and the Wellcome Trust, assisting in the location of UK hospital records. The search facility is very clear but does not respond to use of the return button, so you need to scroll down to 'get results'.

www.ucl.ac.uk/histmed
University College London in conjunction with the Wellcome Trust, features Medical History here, with a list of publications including the quarterly journal 'Medical History' (reduced subscription available to friends of the Wellcome Library) on a subsequent page **www.ucl.ac.uk/histmed/publ.htm**.

www.history.ac.uk/gh/apoths.htm
The Guildhall Library presents an excellent feature, 'Sources for Tracing Apothecaries, Surgeons, Physicians and Other Medical Practitioners at Guildhall Library'.

http://rylibweb.man.ac.uk/data2/spcoll/intsci.html
The John Rylands University Library, Special Collection Guide: History of Science and Medicine is by far the best starting place if you become fascinated by the history of the medical profession.

http://user.itl.net/~glen/doctors.html
'Was Your Ancestor a Doctor?' by Alex Glendinning is very helpful on the subject of where to look for records of a member of the medical profession.

**www.apothecaries.org.uk/society/
index.html**
The Worshipful Society of Apothecaries of London website presents a certain amount of historical background and some beautiful pictures of Apothecaries' Hall.

**www.pharmweb.net/forum/0094/2000/
threads.html**
The PharmWeb History of Pharmacy page is a discussion forum moderated by Greg Higby of the American History of Pharmacy Institute.

www.rpsgb.org.uk/pdfs/tracing.pdf
The Royal Pharmaceutical Society of Great Britain offers this one page of guidance on finding pharmacy records.

**www.davidric.dircon.co.uk/
main.html**
THHOL is full of interesting material about Tower Hamlets, much of it about epidemics of cholera and other illnesses.

**www.paul_smith.doctors.org.uk/
ArchaicMedicalTerms.htm**
Archaic Medical Terms is a website maintained by Paul Smith – brilliantly.

adoptions and illegitimacies

Most orphaned, illegitimate or foundling children (those of no known parentage) sadly ended up in the workhouse. This section should be read in conjunction with the next, on pages 93–95. Don't ignore illegitimacies in your family tree. Sometimes they or workhouse occupants are more successful in life than those born with the proverbial silver spoon.

Georgina Stafford's book *Where to Find Adoption Records* has gone through several editions. The most recent, published in 2002 and vastly increased in size, now costs £20 in paperback (from www.amazon .com), so may be best consulted in libraries. It is basically the most extensive text on the subject of adoption records you will find.

The Office for National Statistics (**www.statistics.gov.uk**) has a series of leaflets you can request from them: Access to Birth Records, The Adoption Contact Register and Information for Adopted People and their Relatives.

One of the little McLaughlin Guides is simply called *Illegitimacy*. Published in 1995, it is worth tracking down, usually at a price of under £2. Try the websites of a few Family History Societies if you are told it is out of print as they may still have copies.

The websites listed here address present-day searches first, and then those for searching in the past. Incidentally, the Salvation Army run a missing persons service but do not trace adoptions.

**www.thesite.org/info/relationships/
adoption/adoption_and_tracing_your_
parents.html**
'Adoption and Tracing Your Parents', from Your Guide to the Real World, is a sensible introductory page, balancing the excitements and anticipated rewards of the quest with warnings about its difficulty and possible disappointments.

**www.uea.ac.uk/swk/research/summaries/
adoptionsearch.htm**
'Adoption, Search and Reunion: The Long Term Experience of Adopted Adults' is the summary of a research project conducted by the School of Social Work and Psychosocial Studies at East Anglia University in conjunction with The Children's Society. Anyone thinking of trying to trace a present-day adoptive connection should possibly read this before embarking on the quest.

www.norcap.org.uk
Norcap is the abbreviated name for the National Organisation for Counselling

Adoptees and Parents. Links include the Rejection Network (for those whose wish for contact is not reciprocated), the Bereavement Network (for those who trace their relatives only to find they are no longer alive) and Forgotten People (support for the partners, spouses and children of adoptees). These titles indicate some of the 'fall-out' that can result from the adoption search.

www.searching4.org
Searching 4 is a free service helping put people looking for birth or adoption family members in touch.

www.afteradoption.org.uk
After Adoption is a registered charity, with many regional branches, helping adopted persons trace relatives, offering counselling and facilitating contact. There is a link to the TalkAdoption helpline.

www.baaf.org.uk
BAAF Adoption and Fostering is a current service.

www.familyrecords.gov.uk/adoptionmain.htm
In this page Family Records divides adoptions under three categories, which are England and Wales, Scotland, and Northern Ireland.

www.statistics.gov.uk/nsbase/registration/adoptions.asp
The National Statistics Office holds and issues adoption certificates. The Adopted Children Register, maintained by the Registrar General, contains a record of every person adopted through a court in England and Wales. Index items include 'Access To Birth Records' and 'Adoption Contact Register'; the latter being the process where adopters and adoptees can explore whether contact would be welcome.

www.adoptionireland.com/index.htm
This visually 'loud' website leads to Irish adoption records past and present.

www.coram.org.uk

The famous Coram Family Foundation has been rescuing destitute and disadvantaged children since 1739, when the Foundling Hospital was established by Thomas Coram. It still runs an adoption service among other functions. There is some historical material here, with a link to the Foundling Museum.

workhouse records

Our ancestors suffered from poverty as much as we do, but sadly the consequences were usually more severe. In the Middle Ages the average township or village was smaller, with a lifestyle based on agriculture and settled family units within the parish.

The very old looked after the very young, and those in the middle worked. The parish was the safety net of last resort. The first Poor Law was introduced during the reign of Elizabeth I in 1601, and it collected money from those able to afford a contribution to care for the 'paupers' of the parish. At this stage the poor were still given 'relief' accommodation in people's homes, where they might be cared for in a benevolent manner but were, of course, frequently exploited and maltreated.

As mobility grew, due both to the Acts of Enclosure and the Industrial Revolution and the fact that people moved into the towns for work, it became a matter of concern that some parishes might find themselves supporting undue numbers of the poor. Consequently settlement records became important, since parishes were determined that outsiders should not become a burden.

The law of Settlements and Removals, passed in 1662, has left many records, including indemnity certificates (settlement certificates or discharges), settlement examinations, removal orders from and to parishes, vagrant passes, appeal notices and clerks' accounts in disputed cases.

By the Victorian era the problem had grown, and The Poor Law Union Act of 1834 (followed by The Poor Law Act of 1845 in Scotland) was introduced, obliging those in need of relief to enter workhouses. Workhouses became the dumping ground of orphans, husbandless women (usually with children) and the old. They fed and sheltered people, in return for some form of work, but were often places of great cruelty. The 1834 Act amended the Settlement Act and imposed detailed record-keeping. Before 1834 records are very scanty.

If you manage to identify an ancestor from the Census as a pauper you stand a good chance of being able to track down the relevant records which will give you a lot of personal detail, such as physical characteristics and health records as well as name, place of birth and parentage.

Poor Law records are normally to be found in County Record Offices or, post-1834, in the Public Record Office. See page 34 of the *Family Tree Magazine*, March 2002, ' Internet Resources for Workhouses', and page 64, October 2000, 'Settlement Papers'.

www.pro.gov.uk/pathways/localhistory/gallery2/poorlaw.htm

The PRO's 'gallery' entry for the Poor Law is the best starting place for an explanation of what records you may find. Don't neglect to use the two links at the bottom of the page, which lead to two very relevant leaflets. If you click on the 'Next' button you can read an article about health and sanitary conditions for the poor.

http://users.ox.ac.uk/~peter/workhouse/records.html

Workhouse Records and Archives is a page of links to relevant websites, contributed by Peter Higginbotham. Although there is some brief explanatory material here, and a good list of records you should look for, the page would be of more use if the links went to the relevant material within those websites, rather than to their homepages.

www.fourbears.worldonline.co.uk/poorlaw.html

Fourbears Research is the family website of Mary Hallett, who offers a very useful search facility for the Poor Law Union Database. You enter the name of the parish that interests you to find the name of the town that administered the Poor Law for that parish.

http://proni.nics.gov.uk/records/poor_law.htm

This is the link for Poor Law and Workhouse records in Northern Ireland.

criminals

When pursuing records of a criminal ancestor, you must first understand a bit about the legal system of the period, so please see pages 85–87 where several websites explore the history of the law. This will help you disentangle the various levels at which a criminal might encounter the legal process.

Your chances of finding the court records of such ancestors are probably better if you can identify where they 'ended up', perhaps in a reformatory, transported to the colonies, or at the worst hanged. Such an outcome should lead you back to the relevant court documents, though you should not be disappointed if these don't give a very detailed account of the trial. The earlier these records are found, the more likely they are to be brief and heavily dependent on Latin 'shorthand', giving little explanation.

Identifying where records are held is far from straightforward but records of relatively minor offences will mostly be in local County Record Offices, while records of major crimes tried at the Old Bailey, and of bankrupts, debtors and convicts being transported, are at the Public Record Office. The PRO also holds police records (unlikely to be of much help before the foundation of the Metropolitan Police in 1829) and records of the Irish Constabulary (founded in 1836, later the Royal Irish Constabulary).

www.hmc.gov.uk/sheets/9_CRIME.htm
This Historical Manuscripts Commission page headed 'Sources for the History of Crime and the Law in England' will start you on the quest.

http://learningcurve.pro.gov.uk
The National Archives Learning Curve is aimed at students but the 'Crime & Punishment' pages are informative at any level. The topics addressed can be seen by rolling your cursor over the picture boxes.

http://catalogue.pro.gov.uk/Leaflets/ri2232.htm
The PRO offers a quick route to identifying where records that may help your search are held. As a starting point, you need to know a county and approximate date.

http://tarlton.law.utexas.edu/lpop/etext/completenewgate.htm
The Complete Newgate Calendar online. Because it is compiled from several sources, be a little wary of inconsistencies.

www.pro.gov.uk/pathways/FamilyHistory/gallery5/prisoners.htm
This PRO page introduces prison records and offers two onward links: 'Domestic Records: Sources for Convicts and Prisoners, 1100–1986' and 'Transportation to Australia 1787–1868.' Follow the 'next' buttons at the bottom of each page for further information about Licences and Pardons, Cases in Chancery and the Court of Requests, each offering links to more detailed articles.

www.le.ac.uk/esh/ca26/eh400/sources
Dr Clare Anderson at Leicester University lectures on Convicts and the Colonies, and this page offers a fascinating list of original sources that give an insight into the thinking of the day, in the eighteenth and early nineteenth centuries, when transportation was a common punishment for what would often be considered minor offences nowadays. Incidentally, clicking on the homepage link will only take you to details of the course students at the university can follow.

www.lightage.demon.co.uk/index.htm#BlackSheep

The Black Sheep Index is a gateway to a vast amount of information, mainly about the police but also about crime and criminal records. Select 'Other Sites of Interest' from the links near the bottom of the page for this area of D. Wilcox's fascinating website.

www.outlawsandhighwaymen.com/links.htm

Outlaws and Highwaymen is a well-ordered website by Gillian Spraggs.

www.bucksfhs.org.uk/bsoc0002.htm

This page from the Buckinghamshire Family History Society lists several publications of relevance to the quest, though unfortunately *Criminal Ancestors – A Guide to Historical Criminal Records in England and Wales* by D. Hawkings is apparently out of print.

newspaper records

Newspapers have been published since the seventeenth century, and together with magazines are a wonderful repository of names and the stories connected with them. If your ancestors were in trade they might have taken out advertisements; if they were in the news there might be stories about them. There were birth, marriage and death entries, and in some cases obituaries.

Magazines, such as *The London Gazette* from 1665 onwards, and *The Gentleman's Magazine* from 1731, are full of information. Both of these, as well as *The Times* (on microfilm) are kept at the Public Record Office. Other early periodicals include Blackwood's *Edinburgh Magazine* from 1817 and the *Illustrated London News* from 1843. There is more information about magazines on pages 126–28.

The main repository for newspapers and magazines is the British Library Newspaper

Library at Colindale in north-west London. Before seeking to investigate there, however, you should try a library close to the location you have identified for research, as most will keep periodicals of local relevance. You would also do well to consult Rosemary Southey's article '18th Century Newspapers for Historians' in the March 2001 issue of *Family Tree Magazine*.

Palmer's Index to *The Times*, listing articles in every issue of the newspaper from October 1790 to December 1905, is now available on CD-rom at major libraries, such as the Guildhall Library. There are over 3-million entries, giving the date, page and column of the article together with a brief summary of the content.

Edinburgh University offers the same online (**see http://edina.ac.uk/palmers/**) but you need to belong to an academic institution that holds a licence to the Index, and have a password, before you can use this facility. Another subscription can be obtained via History Online (**http://historyonline. chadwyck.co.uk/info/home.htm**), but again is restricted to institutions.

www.bl.uk/collections/newspapers.html
The British Library Newspaper Library has an extensive, well-planned website, although you have to sift out the actual holdings from a lot of material about the Library's collecting policy and management.

www.is.bham.ac.uk/specialcoll/resources_bibilej.htm
The Information Service of the University of Birmingham has this somewhat confusing entry-point headed 'Resources for Archivists and Researchers'. It is worth investigating links to Archival and Bibliographical records.

www.bodley.ox.ac.uk/ilej
The Internet Library of Early Journals is an excellent resource, offering 'The Annual Register', 'Notes and Queries', 'The Builder', and the 'Philosophical Transactions of the Royal Society', as well as the *Gentlemen's*

Magazine and Blackwood's *Edinburgh Magazine* online. You can either 'browse' any of the six titles page-by-page, or use the search facility.

www.london-gazette.co.uk
The *London Gazette*, probably the world's oldest newspaper, has its own website here. If you use the upper part of the left-margin index and scroll down you will find a link to 'Gazette History' which, though not long, offers interesting background reading.

emigration and immigration

In family history terms, the immediate reaction when emigration is mentioned is to think of America. Actually, plenty of people left Britain, and came to Britain, in migrations to and from many different countries at many different periods. To take a couple of examples, the Huguenots fled to England from persecution in France in the seventeenth century (many subsequently went on to America), and many Britons went, first as convicts and later as settlers to Australia.

The Internet resources for exploring this field are massive, presumably because those who trace their ancestry to places far from home were among the first to recognise the value of the World Wide Web for such research.

A good but very condensed introduction to the subject of migration in general is offered by **www.genuki.org.uk/big/Emery Paper.html#Emigrants** where a brief list of books and contact addresses for those exploring British and Irish emigration to the colonies is given. Two of the well-known gateway websites, Cyndi's List and the WorldGenWeb Project, present the researcher with a mass of links to online records for all countries of the world. Find these at:

www.cyndislist.com
From the homepage index select Ellis Island; Immigration & Naturalization or Migration Routes, Roads & Trails.

www.worldgenweb.org
The WorldGenWeb Project is a huge gateway to a mass of international information. Select 'Country Index' and proceed.

www.twrco.co.uk/uk2shop-5.htm
TWR Computing, based in Suffolk, provides genealogical information on CD-rom and this page lists their British and Irish Data CDs, including English Settlers in Barbados 1637–1880, Irish Immigrants to North America 1803–1871 and the Complete Book of Emigrants 1607–1776.

www.port.nmm.ac.uk/ROADS/ subject-listing/inter.html
The National Maritime Museum's greatly improved website offers a page within its Home Port Maritime Information Gateway, where you can 'Browse International Relations and Migration'. Each link (to subjects such as The Mayflower Voyage, Australian Immigrant Ships, the Indian Navy and Whatever Happened to the British Empire?) leads to a postcard-size description of the website or web-page you have chosen, and then an onward link connecting to that site. This is a huge list and a very remarkable resource.

www.sog.org.uk/acatalog/SoG_ Bookshop_Online_Migration_68.html
The Society of Genealogists' online bookshop offers a small selection of books on the topic of emigration.

http://freespace.virgin.net/alan.tupman/ sites/index.htm
Alan Tupman's 'Sites with Genealogical Source Material: Emigrants' link at the bottom of the page leads to an excellent shortcut for anyone who has identified the ship on which an ancestor travelled. Select first by country. Full passenger lists are given under ship names.

www.tayvalleyfhs.org.uk/rescent/libcat/mg.htm
Tay Valley FHS has lists of articles and other resources for those studying Scottish migration.

www.frankcass.com/jnls/im.htm
'Immigrants & Minorities' is a journal founded in 1981 by Frank Cass publications. It is possible to search the various issues to see what articles appeared, though not to read the articles themselves online.

www.twrcomputing.freeserve.co.uk/cd600.htm
TWR Computing describes a CD entitled 'Huguenot Settlers in North America and Europe 1600s–1900s', a valuable resource and one that may be ordered online.

www.cityoflondon.gov.uk/leisure_heritage/libraries_archives_museums_galleries/lma/pdf/huguenot_society.PDF
The Huguenot Society of Britain lists its publications on this page.

www.ucl.ac.uk/Library/huguenot.htm
The Huguenot Library has recently moved to 140 Hampstead Road, London NW1. At present its website is limited in scope but this page does explain what records the Library holds, selecting a few major titles and offering onward links to Huguenot websites in other countries.

www.espinet.freeserve.co.uk/book/chapto1.htm
Our Huguenot Ancestors is a personal page by a member of the Espenett family, beginning with good general information about who the Huguenots were and why they were so persecuted.

Ellis Island records

There is probably no better place for embarking on the fascinating topic of emigration to America than Tom Wood's two articles for *Family Tree Magazine* in the November and December issues,

2000. These are 'Ellis Island Gateway to America, Parts I and II'.

It is apparently true to say that 100-million people from the US can claim at least one ancestor who came to the country via Ellis Island. Located in New York Harbour, Ellis Island processed all immigrants from 1892 to 1954. During this period, the majority came from European countries, predominantly from Britain and, especially during the desperate years of the mid-nineteenth century potato famines, from Ireland. Settlers had come in earlier times, too, from the sixteenth century onwards, such as the Pilgrim Fathers, who arrived in the Mayflower in 1620.

Prior to the opening of the Ellis Island reception centre, on 1 January 1892, the Alien Act of 1798 (followed by several later Immigration Acts) had been applied. The handling of immigrants had become a pressing issue and from the moment the centre opened it was processing some 5,000 people a day. The vetting process was both rigorous and daunting. For the new arrivals, exhausted from a long journey, the prospect of failing, and being returned home, as some were made to do, must have been terrifying.

After the centre's final closure in 1954 the Ellis Island buildings became neglected and derelict, but a massive restoration programme began in 1982 and the new Ellis Island Immigration Museum opened in September 1990. Until recently, Ellis Island was not where the immigration records were held. Most, now on microfilm, were held by the US National Archives (see **www.nara.gov/nara/gotonara.html**), though they have now been transferred to the American Family Immigration Center, a new project for the Ellis Island Foundation in conjunction with the Church of Jesus Christ of Latter-day Saints.

Searching Google with the simple words 'Ellis Island' produces 394,000 hits, from which the main ones are selected:

www.ellisisland.org

The American Family Immigration History Center at Ellis Island presents this restrained and easily navigated homepage, with links near the top of the page to Passenger Search, Family Scrapbooks and The Immigration Experience among others. Searching the passenger lists is free, as is registering once you select an individual's record to view. Participation in some areas, such as Family Scrapbooks requires a year's membership subscription, currently $45.

Needless to say, there are other areas here too, such as the Gift Shop and the Wall of Honor. At the bottom of the page is the useful 'prepare for your visit' link, which should be used by anyone going in person.

http://home.pacbell.net/spmorse/ellis/ellis.html

Searching the Ellis Island Database in One Step is Stephen P. Morse's personally created search facility for anyone who finds Ellis Island's own less than easy.

www.ellisisland.com

This is the Ellis Island Immigration Museum's website. If you click on either the Genealogy or History links you will be able to start exploring.

www.nps.gov/stli/servo2.htm

The National Park Service has its own detailed Ellis Island feature.

www.cmp.ucr.edu/exhibitions/immigration_id.html

The California Museum of Photography offers several images under the heading 'New York, NY, Ellis Island – Immigration: 1900–1920'.

obituaries

The International Genealogical Index, that astonishing resource compiled by the Mormons, records births/baptisms and marriages but not (until recently when some have been added) deaths. The Federation of

Family History Societies has undertaken a huge project to fill the gap by creating the NBI, the National Burial Index for England and Wales, which will eventually be a huge resource for family historians.

A similar task is being undertaken in Scotland. The completion of the project will take years, but the first edition, containing over five-million names, mostly from the first half of the eighteenth century, has already been published on two CDs costing £30.

Records of burials are not in themselves obituaries. However, locating a burial, in terms of date and place, may lead to the discovery of a matching obituary.

Some of the earliest and most moving obituaries are found on tombstones, which may on occasion list the achievements of the deceased in some detail. Others can be disappointingly brief, such as the succinct offering on a two-page 'book' memorial in one Fulham churchyard. No attempt is made to match the panegyric to a wife that adorns the first page; instead the opposite leaf merely reads, 'He's gone too'.

Abstracts of wills and probate records may be good sources to trawl for biographical details, as may newspapers and journals carrying obituaries of notable people. But, the great difficulty here is in tracing them.

It is still the case that the online availability of British newspaper obituaries is very disappointing. When will someone make all past obituaries from our long-lived national broadsheets such as *The Times* available?

When surfing for obituaries online, don't get too excited by seeing references to the 'Obituaries *Daily Times*', which is an American publication – unless of course you are looking for forebears across the Atlantic.

Online resources for searching obituaries elsewhere, such as in the US or Australia, are actually somewhat better than our own.

One convenient shortcut is offered by **www.libraryspot.com/ask/askobit.htm**, and in this context **http://the oldentimes.com/deaths.htm** may also be worth trying.

www.ffhs.org.uk/General/Projects/NBI.htm
This FFHS page introduces the National Burial Index and explains its aims. Click on 'Details of Coverage' to view a list of counties, with details of the numbers of parishes and individual records so far collected in each county.

www.rod-neep.co.uk/acatalog/Archive_ CD_Books_Obituaries_149.html
Sir William Musgrave's massive, six-volume work *Musgrave's Obituary* was originally published from 1899 onwards and later made available by the Harleian Society. Now the admirable Rod Neep of Archive CD Books offers it on CD. It indexes obituaries pre-1800 from such sources as the *Gentlemen's Magazine*.

http://historyonline.chadwyck.co.uk/info/ home.htm
History Online offers a link to Palmer's Full Text of *The Times* newspaper online, 1785–1870, with the possibility of a free trial – though this is usually restricted to institutions rather than individuals. There is now a further update, bringing the index forward to 1905.

The same publisher, Chadwyck-Healey, also offers a similar online index to *The Annual Register*, from 1758–2000. To find these, click the Connections button. These CDs are massively expensive to buy (over £4,000), so you need to find them in libraries, such as the Guildhall Library, if you wish to consult them.

www.btinternet.com/~PBenyon/ News_Extracts/Obits_Index_1.html
Extracts from late nineteenth and early twentieth century newspapers, giving obituaries of a selection of figures from political life, the services and the clergy.

chapter 04

when you have got a long way back...

A common question people ask when they hear you are researching your family history is 'how far back have you got?'

As you work backwards the information flows change. Most people can identify their two parents, four grandparents and, with a little investigation, their eight great grandparents. Allowing for about four generations per century (remember it is the average age of parents when children are born, and nothing to do with longevity), you perhaps have a

possible four thousand–ancestors whose lines you could follow by the time you have travelled back in time some three hundred years. Of these, you will be lucky if you have even 10 to work on.

The best hope is that you may find some published data. If you are fortunate enough to find a published pedigree going back a long way it may well lead you to other sources. Remember, though, the presence of data in a publication, particularly on the

Internet, does not necessarily mean it is accurate. Even the most authoritative sources must be evaluated. For example, the 1694 Act of Parliament for the naturalisation of the O'Farrell children (ancestors in our own family who had been born abroad) very clearly names Digna as one of the children, whereas she was actually called Diana.

Joseph Hunter, in the pedigrees he was publishing in the period 1790–1820, is generally recognised to have made many mistakes. Various inconsistencies between different volumes (or even sometimes within the same volume) can be identified when he is presenting the lineage of the same family on two occasions.

The information available from further back inevitably becomes more patchy. Though not many of us are fortunate enough to be in this situation, the search is naturally made easier if you have an unusual surname to work on and may identify a small village as the location from which your family came.

You may then be able to find the relevant parish records which will take you forward.

Many people start to research the history of a place, an activity or a subject (manorial courts, medieval prisons, early regiments or whatever) to flesh out the picture of the life that an ancestor would have been living. You may no longer be discovering anything new about the individual but you are giving him or her a context, and this may be a very rewarding way of bringing your research alive.

By now you will be an experienced researcher and will be using many different sources. You will be learning about topics that are only covered in the most specialist publications – if they have been written about at all!

At the very least, you will be expanding your own knowledge and, who knows, your research may actually contribute something new to the historical record.

Burke's landed gentry

The first edition of Burke's *Landed Gentry* was actually styled *Burke's Commoners* in that its full title was the magnificent *A Genealogical and Heraldic History of the Commoners of Great Britain and Ireland Enjoying Possessions or High Official Rank, but Uninvested with Heritable Honours*. It was produced in four volumes in 1837–38. The first to be called *The Landed Gentry of Great Britain and Ireland* was in fact the second edition of 1847–52. Since then it has gone through 18 editions and has set a standard for genealogical recording that has become the benchmark against which all other works are judged.

It is important to be aware that new editions are not merely revisions bringing each family tree up to date. While there is a core of families that have appeared in every edition, there are also many families featured in the 2,500 pages of each version that are particular to that edition. So, always check.

Good libraries should hold several editions. Alternatively you can try specialist booksellers such as **www.johntownsend.demon.co.uk/page42.html**, who is likely to be offering several different editions for sale at any one time.

There is the likelihood that Burke's will be made fully available online. However, it is probable that only certain editions (maybe only the current edition) will be selected for such a purpose.

CHEST, which describes itself as 'the educational shop window for purchases of software, data, information, training materials and other IT related products' has, according to its own website, **www.chest.ac.uk**, been approached.

Landed Gentry is only one of the whole stable of Burke's titles. These days there are other variants. The first to focus on Ireland was in 1899, and now there is a volume for Scotland as well. In addition, there are the titles listing the noble families of the realm, among which are *Peerage, Baronetage and Knightage*; *Extinct and Dormant Baronetcies of England, Scotland & Ireland* and *Dormant, Abeyant, Forfeited, and Extinct Peerages* (see pages 116–117). Since the sale of Burke's to the Americans and its sad, subsequent decline in terms of offering true assistance to the serious family historian, The Baronage Press (**www.baronage.co.uk**) has become the guardian of both Burke's and Debrett's.

Don't ignore *Walford's County Families*, first produced in 1860, which is very similar to Burke's though less well-known. On the other hand, the very well-known and brilliantly titled *Who's Who* dates back in origin to 1848.

It has spawned a mass of spin-offs, everything from *Who's Who in George Eliot?* to *Who's Who in Japanese Prints?* and even imitators like *Who's Who in Warwickshire?*. The current edition of the original, for 2002, costs £125 but is of virtually no practical use to family historians, and the promising *Who Was Who?* is so selective it is of little genealogical use, but may well be entertaining.

http://proni.nics.gov.uk/records/landed.htm

PRONI, the Public Record Office of Northern Ireland, introduces here its Landed Estates Records, which are a very important part of its holdings. The page ends with a considerable list of some of the major collections.

www.burkes-landed-gentry.com/sites/scotland/sitepages/welcome.asp

Scotland's Past offers a link half way down the homepage to Burke's *Landed Gentry* for Scotland, the first part of the work to be digitised and available for viewing online. It's a website aimed at Americans and subscription is not cheap, but purchasing the book itself costs considerably more, so this may be a useful link for those who are unable to visit a library.

other directories

Following the interest in family history shown by the Victorians, several writers produced 'calendars', directories and similar publications. These tended to have an individual slant, but the distinction between them can be blurred.

County directories include Bailey's, Glover's, Kelly's (also Kelly's Commercial Directory), Pigot's, Slater's and White's. Pigot and Kelly are so well known that copies of their directories for some counties have been reprinted and can be bought as paperbacks. Others are available as CDs. Most libraries will hold some directories, often on microfilm rather than in hard copy, though for the more specialist titles you will have to go to a major depository such as the Guildhall Library.

www.uea.ac.uk/~s300/genuki/NFK/norfolk /gaz-and-dir/examples.shtml
GENUKI uses this page from the University of East Anglia and the example of a sequence of directories for Norfolk to illustrate how directories developed over the years.

www.cityoflondon.gov.uk/leisure _heritage/libraries_archives_museums _galleries/lma/pdf/directories.PDF
The Guildhall Library provides an article explaining what directories are available, how they evolved and what their uses are.

www.victorianlondon.org
Victorian London by Lee Jackson is an absolute treasure-trove, offering *Dickens's Dictionary of London*, by Charles Dickens, Jr., 1879 (shortcut to it via **www.victorianlondon.org/publications/ dictionary.htm**, if you prefer), where you can search by location or by topic. You can also click on Bibliography and find an intriguing list, from which other titles may be read online. Look for *Homes of the London Poor* (1875) by Octavia Hill, *Round London: Down East and Up West* (1894) by Montagu Williams and *The Great Metropolis* (1837) by James Grant, marked as 'Full Text'. The Links

button offers a short but highly relevant list of connections to other websites of interest for those researching Victorian London.

www.rod-neep.co.uk/books/types
Types of Books Useful to Historians & Genealogists is part of Rod Neep's excellent Archive-CD Books website. Click on the 'Directories' link, then scroll down and click on 'directories in more detail'.

http://home.clara.net/dfoster/range.htm
Direct Resources: *c.* 19th Trades Directories for Family Historians, Local Historians and Education starts with a useful description of what directories typically contain and what their use to family historians is. Click on the 'range' link to look at the current list.

www.ancestry.com/search/rectype/directories/ukusdir/main.htm
Early UK & US Directories & Lists, 1680–1830 are offered here by Ancestry.com, with a search facility that actually works quite well. Be warned, though, that the moment it offers you some matches it also asks you to subscribe, at a considerable cost. The list of sources below may offer some hints about where to look.

www.deltacom-design.co.uk/victoriana_historical.htm
The Victorian Era calls itself a 'directory' of all things Victorian. It is a contemporary directory but this page, of historical links, is a very rich hunting ground for anyone seeking to fill out the picture of how their ancestors lived in Victorian times. The Books and Videos link is worth investigating, whereas the Directory itself is dedicated to businesses selling Victorian-style products today.

www.nytimes.com/books/first/c/crook-rise.html
The website of the *New York Times* entertains its readers with literary excerpts under the heading 'Crossing the Line: The Titled and Untitled Aristocracy'; a highly acerbic look at what distinguishes a true aristocrat from a *parvenu*!

heralds' visitations

The Heralds' Visitations were made to establish the rights of families to bear arms (or, if less grand, to be styled esquire or gentleman!) by checking their pedigree. This had the effect of turning the Heralds into the first professional genealogists.

They were sent from the College of Arms into the counties of England from the early sixteenth century (for example in 1530–32 the Visitations were conducted by Thomas Tonge, Norroy, William Fellow, Lancaster Herald and Thomas Benolt, Clarenceux) to the late seventeenth century. The archaic terms 'Norroy', 'Garter', 'Clarenceux' refer to the various Kings of Arms, other officers having fine titles such as 'Portcullis', 'Bluemantle' and 'Rouge Dragon'.

The originals of the Heralds' records are in the College of Arms, with a complete set also being held in the British Library. Many have been published, mostly by the Harleian Society, which shares its Queen Victoria Street, London EC4 address with the College. These publications will also be found in many major libraries, such as the Guildhall Library and SoG.

In 1849 R. Sims published his *Index to the Pedigrees and Arms Contained in the Heralds' Visitations* listed in the British Museum (now the British Library), and this was reproduced by the Genealogical Publishing Company, Baltimore, in 1970 and was again reprinted in 1997. It is currently out of print but may reappear.

www.medievalgenealogy.org.uk/guide/vis.shtml

Who are your British Ancestors? Some notes on English Medieval Genealogy (a most useful website) has this feature on 'Heralds' Visitations and the College of Arms', introducing the exploration of this topic. It starts from a basic description of the Heralds' duties and gives a warning about the meticulousness (or lack of it) with which they carried them out. The 'example' link examines in detail the sixteenth-century pedigree of the Skipwith family. Two links at the bottom of the page go to 'Source material on the Internet' and more general heraldry links.

www.digiserve.com/heraldry

Heraldry on the Internet is a huge gateway website of considerable interest and depth, so don't be put off by the homepage invitations to use heraldry clip-art to create your own coat of arms. The link to Pimbley's Dictionary of Heraldry is handy, as is the feature on Heraldic Symbolism.

www.college-of-arms.gov.uk

The College of Arms website is admirably clear and needs no explanation here. Start from 'About the College of Arms'. The final item in the list on that page is 'Naval, Military and RAF Insignia', which some researchers may be glad to know is available in addition to the more obvious information about family crests and heraldry in general.

http://renaissance.dm.net/heraldry/index.html

Elizabethan Heraldry is an elegant, literary website that goes into fascinating detail about the whole subject, offering transcriptions of contemporary documents as well as many onward links to further information.

www.theheraldrysociety.com/index.htm

The Heraldry Society's web presence is distinctly underwhelming and badly needs both improvement (including deletion of now redundant pages from some presumably earlier, even less adequate incarnation), as well as a more regular updating of things like the 'current programme' page, on which all of the events listed had already happened at the time of viewing. The Society's objective is a good one, however, so until the website is redesigned the best plan is probably to use the following contact details: The Secretary, The Heraldry Society, PO Box 32, Maidenhead, Berks, SL6 3FD, England. Tel/fax: 0118 932 0210.

county histories

County Histories often contain extensive genealogical information about the families who lived in a county and can be a fruitful area for research of earlier times. They are distinct from Directories in being descriptively topographical in approach. However, it is often helpful to research them in conjunction with their more 'telephone-book' style relatives.

The earliest county histories of use to family historians were published in the seventeenth century, such as Burton's *Description of Leicester Shire* published in 1622 and Dugdale's *The Antiquities of Warwickshire* in 1656. These tended to restrict mention of individual families to the significant landed families of the county. In the late eighteenth and early nineteenth century, many more County Histories were published and included mention of lesser families. They covered periods later than those in the Heralds' Visitations (see pages 112–13), which were mostly being carried out in the sixteenth and seventeenth centuries.

Most County Record Offices and major libraries have copies of the volumes relating to their own areas, though only major libraries such as SoG and the British Library hold them for many counties. A good catalogue of existing works then in the British Museum Library, *The Book of British Topography*, was written by John P. Anderson in 1881 and reprinted in facsimile by E.P. Publishing in 1976. A current book of great value to anyone exploring this area of research for the first time is *Guide to English County Histories* edited by C.R. Currie and C.P. Lewis.

It is worth remembering that much useful historical material, stored by county offices, may be held in many forms other than in books. For instance, the County Assessor's or Surveyor's office may contain survey logs and records, as may the Auditors Office. Similarly, County

Commissioners' Minutes Books, Circuit Court Order Books and a whole host of minor documents, even down to the level of hand-drawn maps for the purposes of land registry and the settling of boundary disputes, may be of use to you. See also the feature on County Record Offices (pages 133–134).

http://rylibweb.man.ac.uk/data2/spcoll/county

The John Rylands University Library lists some 500 books in its County Histories Collection. Making notes of the selected titles listed here would be useful for anyone wondering what to look for when exploring these resources.

www.sog.org.uk/acatalog/SoG_Bookshop _Online_Local_History_61.html

The Society of Genealogists' Bookshop lists a good number of titles, mostly under £20, of relevance to those researching local history. Among them is the Currie and Lewis title mentioned before.

www.englandpast.net

The Victoria County History, which began in 1899 in the last years of Queen Victoria's reign, is still being developed over a century later. Two hundred and twenty volumes have already been produced and many, many more are still in the pipeline. Some counties are listed as being 'dormant', whereas some already have websites up and running. From the homepage there is a link to The Association of British Counties (**www.abcounties.co.uk**), a campaigning website devoted to the fight against losing the traditional county structure of Great Britain. It contains some interesting historical background material.

www.local-history.co.uk/groups/index.html

The Local History Directory is a contemporary resource, listing local history societies nationwide, and these may be of real assistance to any family historian, especially those researching in counties with which they are not personally familiar.

the nobility

If you manage to trace your ancestry back a few hundred years, there is a realistic chance that you may find a titled person among your forebears. This will generate two consequences. One is that there is a great deal of written source material that you can access and research becomes very easy. The other is that you will be given a direct route to ancestors of very early date, as most of the peerage is very well recorded. For a scholarly overview of the history of the aristocracy throughout Europe, *The European Nobility, 1400–1800* by Jonathan Dewald, now available in paperback, cannot be bettered.

There are two central works that will help you trace the descent of British noble families. Debrett's and Burke's are both publications of considerable longevity and stature, though not the only volumes of their kind. For example, early competitors include *The Baronetage of England* by Kimber and Johnson (1771) and *The Dormant and Extinct Baronage of England* by Banks (1807). Eventually, however, Debrett's and Burke's led the field.

Don't forget that they have both come out in numerous editions over the years, and contain different information depending on the date of publication. It is not safe to assume that the most recent edition will be the best. It could almost be argued that no current edition is likely to be the most valuable to the family historian.

Debrett's *Peerage and Baronetage* appeared most recently in 2000 and is, says *The Times*, 'more and more indispensable as a work of reference'. It costs £250, or twice that sum leather-bound, so you may prefer to consult it in a library.

Where Debrett's stands alone, Burke's *Peerage, Baronetage and Knightage*, to give it its older title, is by no means the only title in Burke's list. Others include *Extinct and*

Dormant Baronetcies of England, Scotland & Ireland and *Dormant, Abeyant, Forfeited, and Extinct Peerages*. Burke's current *Peerage and Gentry*, now in its 106th edition, has recently become available online:

www.burkes-peereerage.net/sites/ peerageandgentry/sitepages/home.asp

Burke's Peerage Online is offered to internet users, for a fee, quoted here in dollars: $99 for a year's use, and $25 for 24 hours. Using Burke's (or indeed Debrett's) takes a little work on your part, and a certain amount of practice, so, if you do decide to go the subscription route, we strongly advise that you familiarise yourself with an edition in hard copy first.

www.history.ox.ac.uk/currentunder/ bibliographies/mods-os-english_nobility. pdf

Honour Moderations in Modern History: Nobility and Gentry in England 1560–1660 is part of a history degree syllabus at Oxford University. Should you wish to explore the subject in real depth, you could start with the reading list here.

www.titleresearch.ndo.co.uk/start.html

Title Research will research whether the title of any particular village or location is for sale, will forge for you an 'Honourable Member's hallmark silver medal' and claim that you will be eligible to attend luncheons held in the House of Lords by the Landed Gentry Society 'subject to availability'. You pay a deposit of £500, refundable if no suitable title is found, and £5,000 to purchase a title, or twice that sum if one with Royal connections is secured.

www.nobility.co.uk

Noble Titles offer a similar service and rates start from £3,500.

www.aristocratic-titles.co.uk

Aristocratic Titles is another option along the same lines, insisting that a title 'says more than a Gold American Express card'.

royalty

Almost all of us are descended from King Edward I, it's just that we can't prove it. After all, he lived about 30 generations ago and, even if there were only two children per subsequent family, he would have 2000-million descendants today, while there are actually only some 60-million of us. Each one of us, on the other hand, has, within only 10 generations, 1024 direct ancestors. There is bound to be some overlap somewhere.

Edward I had ten children. Many children didn't survive and lines intermarried, so the true number of his descendants is much fewer than the theoretical number. Ruvigny in his five-volume *The Plantagenet Roll* records about 50,000 descendants of Edward III alive in 1905.

It has, of course, been the habit for most of time that royalty should only marry with royalty, which means that international marriages have been a major factor in British royal lineage. As a result, any genealogical research involving royalty will want to use the *Almanac de Gotha* (see below), which is a study of all European royalty.

www.royal.gov.uk/output/Page1.asp

The Official Website of the British Monarchy is a curious mixture of intimacy and actual distance, using an approachable style and oddly detached content. A couple of anodyne paragraphs tell the story of each stage of the monarchy's history, but not providing the meaty account that might be expected.

www.britannia.com/history

Britannia is, as it says, America's Gateway to the British Isles, and its History Department is detailed and well laid out; however, the emphasis tends to be on the earlier centuries. Arthurian legend features heavily, but with a bit of digging you will unearth real riches. There are no apparent shortcuts through the mass of material. For instance, the only way to read Peter Williams' good 'Narrative History of England' is apparently to work successively through all eight chapters. With no search facility on offer, it can be slow, and there is a regular need to delete flashing advertisements and prize offers. If you do it often enough they will go away. Do persist, as there is much here to enjoy.

http://gsteinbe.intrasun.tcnj.edu/royalty/royalty.html
European Royalty During World War II by Glenn A. Steinberg contains many good links to the royal houses of Europe.

www.eurohistory.com/main.htm
European Royal History is the rather odd website of Arturo Béeche, which is 'intended to be an historian's paradise'. It will need to build up a good deal before it becomes that, but it may be worth a visit.

www.xs4all.nl/~kvenjb/introduction/introduction.htm
Welcome to my Royalty in History site, is a site about non-Royal behaviour of Royals in history!

www.royalty.nu
The World of Royalty website homepage presents an eclectic index but, if you scroll down, you will find a number of links to British Royalty. The approach is to describe the individual monarchs rather than to take a wider view, but the site is a serious one and various bibliographies are offered, too.

www.cyndislist.com/royalty.htm
Cyndi's List Royalty & Nobility page offers the usual mass of links and is a fundamental resource for any history lover.

http://worldroots.com/brigitte/royal/royaloo.htm
Worldroots hosts European Royalty and Nobility, the website of Brigitte Gastel Lloyd. Exploration is easy and rewarding.

www.almanachdegotha.com/main_page.htm
The *Almanach de Gotha*, published in almost every year since 1763, has its website here, though the online information is limited.

coats of arms and the college of arms

It is a misconception that having a particular surname entitles you to use the Coat of Arms (properly 'armorial bearings'), which might have been granted to a previous holder of the name. This is emphatically not the case. Also, the often-misused term 'crest' refers to part of the coat of arms, not the whole thing. These points and many others need explanation and understanding before you inquire about any entitlement you may have.

Coats of Arms are granted by the College of Heralds to an individual, and once granted will descend through the male line. By courtesy they may be used by a man's daughters, but can only be passed on by a daughter in the event that she has no brothers, and hence is armigerous in her own right. In that instance, her arms can then be quartered with those of her husband.

Do be warned that there are too many websites who will be delighted to draw up for you so-called 'authentic' coats of arms and charge you very considerable sums for doing so. They will then offer you all sorts of merchandise bearing your 'personal crest', from artificially aged parchment to mugs and golfing umbrellas.

www.sog.org.uk/leaflets/arms.html
The Society of Genealogists publish online this leaflet no. 15 entitled 'The Right to Arms'. There are no links, no illustrations and no special offers – just good, solid information about who may have armigerous rights and how to find out. The text contains references to a number of books that will expand your knowledge and understanding of the subject.

www.bl.uk/collections/wider/heraldry.html
The British Library's Heraldry Reference Sources are divided under General, Great Britain, Europe and Russia. One link goes to the College of Arms, whose website is

described below, while the other references are to books rather than to websites. 'About the College of Arms' is the most informative link, leading to features such as 'How the College of Arms Works', 'Some Past Heralds' and 'Proving a Right to Arms by Descent' and 'Genealogical Research.' It is also worth looking at Frequently Asked Questions.

www.college-of-arms.gov.uk

The College of Arms is the official repository of the coats of arms and pedigrees of English, Welsh, Northern Irish and Commonwealth families. It does also hold copies of the records of Ulster King of Arms, the originals being held in Dublin.

www.ihgs.ac.uk/index.php

The Institute of Heraldic and Genealogical Studies, headed by the inimitable Cecil Humphery-Smith, is a basic resource for all researching in the heraldry field.

www.twrcomputing.freeserve.co.uk/cd368.htm

TWR Computing can offer information about British and American Coats of Arms on CD-rom.

www.nameseekers.co.uk/arms1.htm

Nameseekers offer Computer Drawn Coats of Arms, for those completely wedded to their PCs, an entertaining though hardly authentic facility.

www.freecoatsofarms.com

Free Coats of Arms is the website of James P. Wolf and, in a world where only too many people are prepared to fleece you of large sums of money to create a spurious coat of arms, this is pretty harmless by comparison. A lot of actual devices are viewable online, though there is access to little explanatory material. You can download a limited number of images free of charge – with no promises that you have identified the right ones, of course.

chapter 05

general advice about other sources

The last chapter of this book may help you from a practical point of view. For instance, it explains a little about maps, magazines and books, before going on to look at how you should approach the use of certain major resources, such as the Public Record Office, the Family History Centre, the Society of Genealogists and the Guildhall Library as well as those in your local area, like County Record Offices and Mormon Family History Centres. If you have not made use of these before, then a little advance preparation is always rewarded,

especially in terms of saving you time, or at least preventing you from wasting it.

If you can't get to all the repositories you would like to visit in person, then there are people who will do research for you, for a fee. But there are also some people who will exchange documents and other material, who will search sites such as churchyards in localities you are researching (usually in exchange for you doing the same for them in your own area) and who will even collect material for you free of charge. Building good relationships with other family historians is never a bad idea. Contacting such people has been greatly assisted by the advent of the Internet.

The book ends with some minor aids, to help you tackle some of the problems that all family historians encounter, like the reading of Latin, the peculiarities of calendar changes and the difficulty of reading early handwriting. Finally, there is a list of addresses and telephone numbers for the major organisations used by all family historians.

If you have worked your way through this book in a more-or-less sequential way, you will by now have noticed that certain websites keep reappearing. The most obvious ones are GENUKI, the Society of Genealogists, the Public Record Office and the Guildhall Library, the Family History Centre, the IGI (Mormon Index) and the Federation of Family History Societies. There are some other big 'gateways' you may have come to like, such as Cyndi's List which, despite recently adopting advertisement banners, does seem to be performing its unrivalled function as a virtual library of online genealogical material. If you are a regular buyer of books or CD-roms you may find you go to Amazon, Abebooks or Archive-CD-books.

It would be a good idea to save a short list of the websites you visit most often in your 'favorites' or 'bookmarks' file. Opening a special internal folder and naming it Family History or something similar is advisable: when you are surfing in search of your ancestors, as opposed to using the Internet for other purposes, you will then have shortcut links to these websites literally at your fingertips.

If in making this suggestion, we are teaching our grandmothers to suck eggs, we apologise, but good organisation is one of the keys to successful research and you may find that a plan of this sort is very helpful.

maps and gazetteers

Maps can be works of great artistry and beauty, as well as encapsulating the history of an area. Early maps are those printed in the fifteenth century. Saxton, Speed and Morden are names well known to cartographers. They usually portrayed the counties (52 in England and Wales, 33 in Scotland), but these maps do not provide much detail.

The Tithe Redemption Maps (see pages 63–64) did provide detail, as did the London maps of Braun and Hogenberg (c. 1560), Ogilby and Morgan (1676) and Hawgood (1799). In this context, topographical prints and paintings give as much information as early maps. A notable example is Wynegaerde's image of London, published about 1540. For maps or images of London, do explore the exquisite publications of the London Topographical Society.

The first Ordnance Survey maps were at a scale of 1 mile to the inch, and were published from about 1805 as part of the first series, which was of questionable accuracy. The second series, published from 1840 was significantly better, and was accompanied by the 6-inch survey, to be followed by the 25-inch survey in 1853.

Gazetteers are always useful in identifying where places are. If your ancestor was born in Sutton, in which of the 36 'Suttons' (simply meaning South Town) in England and Wales are you searching? And what about the further 62 places in which Sutton is part of the name?

An early gazetteer, and probably the best, is Lewis's *Topographical Directory*, divided into four volumes for England, Scotland, Wales and Ireland. Also good for England and Wales is Wilson's *Imperial Gazetteer* of 1870.

Among more specialist ones are Clarke's *New Yorkshire Gazetteer or Topographical Dictionary* of 1828. These are particularly useful in building up the picture of a place, as they may give population figures, who owned the patronage of the living and what local industry there was.

Remember that while places don't move, county boundaries do. After searching for years to identify a 'Norton' in Derbyshire (a seventeenth century reference), we finally found it just into Yorkshire. This can have great significance, because it may identify the County Record Office holding the relevant registers.

The *Historian's Guide to Early British Maps*, edited by Helen Wallis and Anita McConnell, is a guide to the location of British maps before 1900.

www.bodley.ox.ac.uk/guides/maps/mroomnf.htm

The Bodleian Library's Map Room is a clear website with 'Cool Map Links' and 'Map Images' as probably the two most useful areas to explore. There is much online information, both written and visual, here.

www.cartography.org.uk/Pages/Useful.html

The British Cartographic Society's website has a particularly good page of relevant links.

www.pro.gov.uk/ancestorsmagazine/issue4.htm

The Public Record Office's most major map holdings are explained, with the warning that they do not form one, cohesive 'map collection'.

www.multimap.com
www.streetmap.co.uk

Multimap and Streetmap are both ideal websites for locating any present-day address, with straightforward search facilities that will respond to minimal details such as a street name or a postcode.

www.history.ac.uk/maps/whatfind.html

The WWW-Virtual Library gateway offers links on the history of cartography.

www.jams.swinternet.co.uk/Inventories1.htm

Gazetteer of Buildings by Area, by Jean Manco, is a page introducing a mass of relevant sources, such as Pevsner on CD-rom and the Images of England website, which is in the process of putting images of all Britain's listed buildings on CD. This is part of the Sources for Buildings History website at: **www.jams.swinternet.co.uk**

www.gwp.enta.net/index.htm

The Domesday Collection of Maps is illustrated here, selling fifty hand-coloured historical maps of considerable beauty.

magazines: past and present

This chapter should be read in conjunction with the feature about Newspaper Records (pages 97–99), the less-than-clear delineation between the two being due to the fact that the earliest magazines were more like 'news' providers.

The circulation of regular magazines for reading has a long history. The first is normally considered *The Gentleman's Magazine* (or *Monthly Intelligencer*), first published in 1731. It listed births, marriages, deaths and promotions (not only in the military). You can search the magazine at **www.bodley.ox.ac.uk/ilej/journals/srchgm.htm**.

Many other publications succeeded it, such as *The Edinburgh Review*, *The Universal Magazine* and *The London Review*. The content of these publications was a mixture of literary (most Dickens novels were first published in magazine form), current affairs, and instruction (for example, *The Farmer's Companion*: a Receipe (sic) to cure the Rot in Sheep, February 1748).

Later, specialist magazines started appearing, though most did not achieve very long runs. However, they illustrate the great interest in genealogy, even in Victorian times. They included *The Genealogist* (1877–1921), *Miscellanea Genealogica et Heraldica* (1868–1938), *Collectanea Topographica* (1834–43), *Topographer and Genealogist* (1846–58) and *The Ancestor* (1902–25), all of which have been indexed by Stuart Raymond in a useful series of volumes published by the FFHS.

We now look at contemporary magazines, some readable online, some not (or not yet).

www.family-tree.co.uk
www.family-tree.co.uk/sister.htm

The incomparable *Family Tree Magazine* and its sister publication, *Practical Family History*, have their online presence here, with articles combining informative but lightly written background articles with research opportunities and references. These cannot be read online. Links and More Links, from the Family History Resources tab at the top of the page, are valuable lists.

www.sog.org.uk/acatalog/SoG_Bookshop _Online_Magazines_328.html
www.sog.org.uk/acatalog/SoG_Bookshop _Online_General_Magazines___Journals_ 63.html

Apologies for the long URLs, but these two pages introduce the Society of Genealogists' own two magazines, *The Genealogists' Magazine* and *Computers in Genealogy*, as well as half a dozen other useful periodicals.

www.ffhs.co.uk/shop/pages/fhnd.htm

The Federation of Family History Societies' magazine, *Family History News & Digest* is displayed here, but is not readable online.

www.spub.co.uk/protgi/links13.html

Peter Christian's useful page is headed 'The World of Family History' and lists both Print Magazines and Journals and Online Publications.

www.sagepub.co.uk/frame.html?
www.sagepub.co.uk/journals/details/j0173
.html

Sage Publications of Canada present this link for the 'Journal of Family History', which they describe as 'scholarly research from an international perspective concerning the family as a historical form'.

http://uk.dir.yahoo.com/arts/
humanities/history/genealogy/
magazines/

This page from the massive Yahoo! Directory introduces a number of online magazines, mainly American, including 'Everton's Genealogical Helper', 'Family Chronicle' and 'Heritage Quest'.

www.rootsforum.com/newsletter/
index.htm

'Eastman's Online Genealogy Newsletter' retains its standing as one of the best of the emailed journals. Others include 'Rootsweb Review' (**www.rootsweb. com**) and Rob Thompson's 'UK-Family History

News' (**www.genuki.org.uk/ news**), for all of which back issues remain readable, too.

www.121zone.com/pages/Society/
Genealogy/Magazines_and_Ezines

This page from 121zone offers links to a number of relevant journals, not all online, again mostly of American origin.

www.iwm.org.uk/lambeth/
famhist5.htm

The Imperial War Museum emphasises the importance of some journals you might not think of consulting, such as regimental, ship, squadron, station or trench journals, for tracing records of service personnel. The only onward link is to the Museum's own Department of Printed Books, but from this further links are available.

www.jgsgb.org.uk/journal1.htm

'Shemot' is the journal of the Jewish Genealogical Society of Great Britain.

books

Books are the route to almost all knowledge, and they are also one way of paupering yourself. You need not buy them though, as nearly all books can be borrowed from your local library. If a volume is so obscure that your library cannot obtain it for you, you may still consult it in one of the specialist libraries, such as the Society of Genealogists' Library or the British Library.

Books currently in print can be bought from specialist sellers such as SoG or the FFHS, from bookshops in the high street such as Waterstone's or Borders, or online from Amazon (see **www.amazon.co.uk**). In this last instance, you will probably find that the cost of postage is easily defrayed by the discount on the selling price. This becomes especially true when you order several books at once.

Apart from the advantage of not having to visit a bookshop in person, you will find that Amazon never has to apologise for being 'out of that particular title at the moment' (unless the book is actually out of print). It also offers reviews of most titles, often accompanied by star-rated customer reviews as well. You pay by secure transaction credit card, and most books will be delivered very promptly, usually within two or three days. In this respect, the high street bookshop asking you to wait two to three weeks has some catching up to do!

If you need (or are interested in) antiquarian books and you succumb to the lure of ownership, there are numerous routes to finding a specific volume. There are many book dealers in specialist subjects who sell via regularly published catalogues, though some may charge you for a subscription to their list. See **www.booksellers.org.uk/links**, where The Booksellers' Association website has numerous links to all areas of the UK book trade, including several book-finding services.

A recently developed, highly efficient way of finding specific antiquarian books is via the Internet. There are several book portals, but we suggest you start with Abebooks, which brings together the lists of many antiquarian and second-hand book dealers, making it possible for you to search many more collections than you could ever hope to visit in person.

These days, however, many reference books are available on microfiche, and this is a very cheap and compact way to acquire a library. With the increasing use of computers, the modern format is CD-rom. Using the most up-to-date Acrobat Reader for those CDs using a pdf format, the book becomes searchable, and you can use the index with a page finder facility.

There are many suppliers, such as Archive CD Books (**www.archivecdbooks.com**). They warn that books in this form must be handled even more carefully than 'pressed' CDs – the sort you may buy for your hi-fi.

The NSTC (The Nineteenth Century Short Title Catalogue) lists books published between 1801 and 1919 on CD, and it can be consulted at the websites of the many contributing universities. See also **http://c19. chadwyck.co.uk** and click on 'Nineteenth Century "live" on the WWW'.

www.abebooks.com
Abebooks (the Advanced Book Exchange) has an eminently clear website, with a search facility that offers search by author, title or – very usefully – keyword, as well as another advanced search. Although many prices are given in US dollars, many titles are actually being offered by UK-based booksellers. Be sure to check these before scrolling past them.

http://bubl.ac.uk/link/r/rarebooks. htm
The BUBL Catalogue of Internet Resources has this page on Rare Books, with good links.

specialist booksellers' catalogues

How do you know what you don't know? If that sounds an idiotic question, don't worry. It's actually a relevant one when you start making use of specialist book catalogues.

There are plenty of booksellers who still, despite the advent of the Internet, continue to sell books on specific topics from bricks-and-mortar premises, and via the services of what we used to call the Post Office.

Most will send you their catalogues free of charge, though a few may charge you a modest subscription. Libraries and local Family History Societies will have lists of such booksellers, and others will be found advertised in *The Antiquarian Book Review* and *Family Tree Magazine*, for example.

One of the values of book catalogue lists is that they don't only sell books. Some sell maps, trade directories and obscure minor reference works and all kinds of historical documents, from old wills to Acts of Parliament.

They may specialise in family history, but once you open out your own research you will make equally useful discoveries among the booklists of historical or topographical specialists, and perhaps in places where the topic is even more closely defined, such as military history or industrial archaeology.

Don't be too dismissive of those booksellers who advertise themselves as dealing in second-hand, as opposed to antiquarian, books. Many publications that are of relevance to family historians are not necessarily beautifully produced tomes worthy of the antiquarian's shelves.

The temptations presented by catalogue lists can be immense and unless you have limitless funds at your disposal you need to be strong-willed about how much you spend. If you are concerned that you may be being asked to pay over the odds for a book, you may find it useful to use the online antiquarian and second-hand bookshops to compare the price of books that you are interested in.

It is important to keep old booklists, space permitting, because they are exceptionally useful as bibliographies of books on specialist subjects.

It is also important to remember that your local library can obtain nearly all books that you require, provided you are prepared to wait a little. There are very few titles that are so obscure that a local library cannot borrow them on your behalf from a more major repository.

In the case of very rare books, however, you may not be permitted to remove the book from the library and may instead have to consult the book you are interested in during library hours.

www.bookweb.co.uk/booksellers/a.htm
Bookweb lists large numbers of booksellers, most with descriptions of their specialisms.

www.haybooks.com/index.htm
HayBooks.com is the website of the international 'world's largest concentration of bookshops selling old and out-of-print books'.

www.abebooks.com
www.alibris.com
www.bibliology.com
www.biblion.com
The above are just four of the many websites offering second-hand or antiquarian books for sale online.

www.paperantiques.co.uk
Paper Antiques (on our latest visit offering 'catch pennies' or broadsheet ballads of the sort that were handed out in the streets to tell of recent noteworthy or criminal events) is a website where serious temptation is put your way!

using county record offices and libraries

Although the terms and meanings are clear, this area covers a considerable range of resources. Many large city libraries contain a local history centre, an archives and local studies centre or even a local family history unit.

A County Record Office is not necessarily in a large town, and is usually found at a separate location from the library facilities. For example, the North Yorkshire County Record Office is in a fairly small building in Northallerton (not in York), while the Lancashire County Record Office is in a large new building in Preston.

On the whole County Record Offices do not contain large collections of books. They are equipped with maps, microfilms and local records, such as those relating to the parishes and to matters such as taxation.

You should always make an appointment if you wish to consult the records, as the number of microfilm readers may be limited, or certain records may be unavailable on certain days. A discussion with the helpful staff about what you are researching will usually lead to material being prepared in advance and waiting ready for your visit.

Library facilities are more book-based and seldom need an appointment. However, it is still worth ringing up if you are travelling any distance because some have Census, IGI or even BDM film, for which a microfilm reader might need to be booked in advance.

Establishing what is held where is always worthwhile, since the approximate divisions may not always apply. For example, in the local history section of York City Library they do in fact hold many parish records that have been printed in book form, but for the complete set one still needs to go to Northallerton CRO. The local Census returns, however, are in Northallerton town library.

Some CROs have extremely good web sites, such as Wolverhampton, on **www.wolverhamptonarchives. dial.pipex.com**, which gives particularly good links to where different records are held. Again, finding out in advance is important, particularly as the records are sometimes moved around when county boundaries are moved (or new counties created – see the section on maps). For example, Measham was in Derbyshire in 1870 (*Wilson's Gazetteer*), but in Leicestershire in 1959 (*Oxford Dictionary of Place-names*), and the records are now in Leicester CRO.

www.hmc.gov.uk/archon/archon.htm
ARCHON is the Historical Manuscripts Commission archive website. It is not the easiest site to use but contains quite a bit of useful information if you can get at it.

www.englandpast.net/record.html
'Where Next? County Record Offices and Local Studies Libraries' is a marvellously useful shortcut to these bodies listed by county. Don't believe their advice that ARCHON is a better source for finding this information. If you try to extract it from that source you will understand!

using mormon family history centres

Mormon Family History Centres will be among the first places you use in your research, certainly just as early as the Family Records Centre in London. The advantage is that there is probably a Family History Centre not too far away, wherever you live in the UK. The amount of information they offer besides the International Genealogical Index (IGI), which is their chief claim to fame, is variable depending on how big they are.

FHCs are usually stocked with a number of microfiche readers and possibly several microfilm readers as well, according to what records besides the IGI they hold. Typically, the IGI is on microfiche, in other words in card index format rather than as reels of film.

Larger FHCs mostly offer the IGI on CD-rom. This version is more up-to-date and the search facility is much more powerful. Notably, when you input a name using the CDs you are offered all matches from the whole country you are searching, rather than county-by-county, which is the case with the fiches. On the other hand you can still refine your CD search by county, so you lose nothing by going the CD-route if you can.

While the IGI is taken from parish records, some FHCs also have civil registration BDMs, – in this case on microfilm rather than microfiche – and possibly some Census returns. As for additional records they may hold, this varies from one FHC to another. On the whole, however, you should expect them to have very few books, if any at all.

Through your local Mormon FHC you have intellectual access to the far more extensive record holdings at the headquarters of the Church of Jesus Christ of the Latter-day Saints in Salt Lake City. This is an incredible repository of every imaginable sort of record, which is assembled from many different parts of the world, though obviously with a preponderance of American material.

Many local Family History Societies in the UK run trips there. Alternatively, you can arrange to borrow records from Salt Lake City for delivery a month or so later, for use in your local FHC.

FHC opening hours are limited, depending on when volunteers are available to staff them. Perhaps they are open something like two afternoons and three evenings a week.

Visits to FHCs are always by appointment because of the necessity to book a microfiche reader in advance. Your time, once booked on a reader, is probably for that session, perhaps for a period of two to three hours. In busy areas where there is pressure on use of the centre, you may find that this means you have to wait a few weeks for an appointment.

Remember to take a notebook (possibly indexed in address-book style if you find this helpful) in which to record what you find, and do make a note of the sources quoted for each record. If you are to carry out your family history research meticulously, you should use the data you collect here only as a prompt for where to find and check the original record.

When you use a Family History Centre for the first time you will probably be shown round by a volunteer, who will be very willing to help if, for example, you have never used a microfiche reader or CD-rom before.

Do remember that the staff are all volunteers, so be polite and grateful for whatever assistance they can give.

using the family records centre

The Family Records Centre is a free-standing branch of the Public Record Office but should definitely be used first, reserving a visit to the PRO itself for a much later stage in your research. It is a wonderful brand new resource, purpose-built in Myddelton Street, London EC1, and it brings together BDMs formerly in St Catherine's House, Census returns from Portugal Street, and some other information, including wills of early date from Chancery Lane and later ones from Somerset House.

Being built and staffed in response to a recognised rapidly increasing need for good public access to the most frequently used family history records, the FRC is very user-friendly. The staff are trained to be able to tell you where things are, and the vast numbers of microfiche readers available mean that you can turn up and expect to be able to start using one immediately. There is no need to make a prior appointment.

On the ground floor near the entrance you will find the shop and the ranks of massive ledgers that you will need to use to identify relevant BDMs. Make a note of any certificates of which you wish to order copies.

In the basement are the locker rooms and the cafeteria. On the first floor are a series of introductory display panels, the IGI (on microfiche and CD) and wills and nineteenth century Census records on microfilm. Here you will also find a number of books, mainly relating to those records, but not forming a general reference library as such. The information you can obtain here is good, and the staff are knowledgeable.

Opening hours are extensive, though rather than list them here we prefer to direct you to the website (**www.familyrecords.gov.uk**) for the latest information. You will find that you meet with a friendly and helpful welcome.

Even so, you should expect to take some time to 'bed in' and learn your way around. You are not likely to be fully effective on your first visit.

using the society of genealogists and the guildhall library

The Society of Genealogists and the Guildhall Library are not too far apart geographically, being in London EC1 and EC2 respectively. The Family Records Centre (FRC) is also not far away, and it should normally be used first, before moving on to more detailed resources.

SoG is in Charterhouse Buildings, near the Barbican, in premises that it shares with GOONS, the Guild of One-Name Studies. It is an incredible resource on several floors. The film reading room, for consulting records on both microfilm and microfiche, contains not only Census returns and BDMs but so much else besides. It is the extent of these additional holdings that distinguishes SoG from, for instance, the FRC. In fairness to other users, you should probably reserve it mainly for consultation of these records rather than using it as a place of preliminary research.

On the first and second floors are the libraries, stacked with rare books and documents, covering all sorts of unusual topics. There are also substantial collections of County Records, arranged by county, many not to be accessed elsewhere – for instance not even in the Record Offices of the counties concerned.

Parish records, where they exist in book form, are also held here, as are near-complete runs of Army and Navy Lists. In addition to the English and Welsh data you will find extensive Scottish and Irish records as well.

Among the great values of SoG are its own, self-generated indexes, which really should be used. By checking names in these indexes, you will find out if there are holdings for those names, and you can sometimes come upon wonderful discoveries, thanks to the meticulousness with which they have been compiled and maintained over the years.

The big advantage of coming here is the opportunity to consult rare books that you are unlikely to find elsewhere, with such a wide range held in a single place.

Preparation for your visit is useful; if you can, try to scan the holdings remotely in advance. It is not as vital, however, as it is for some other record repositories. Items you request arrive quickly, or in many cases you can simply go to the shelves and collect them yourself.

SoG requires membership but non-members can buy day tickets to use the library. The staff are both helpful and knowledgeable, but do remember that the majority are volunteers simply doing their job for the love of it.

guildhall library

The Library is in Aldermanbury, to the side of the Guildhall itself. The main library on the ground floor, facing you as you enter, contains complete runs of the Harleian Society publications, almost complete runs of London Directories (the collection in general is fairly London-centric) and such documents as Acts of Parliament. Palmer's Index to *The Times* newspaper is available on CD-rom, and the IGI is also held.

On the upper floor there is a map room and microfiche and microfilm readers for Guild information, such as parish records. There is a very good helpdesk, excellent indexes, and books or documents are produced promptly in response to requests. No advance booking is needed.

You may find, however, that it is busy at lunchtime, as people dash in from their offices to snatch a few more minutes of research time.

using the public record office

The Public Record Office is the most magical resource, and it's all for free. It is the national repository for records, and almost the only drawback is that one has to go to Kew. However, it is definitely worth the trip. The staff are friendly and knowledgeable, and the opportunities are limitless.

At the first visit it is intimidating, and the compulsory introductory tour, lasting about 20 minutes, is necessary. It is, however, still hard to remember all that you are shown. You should study the very helpful topic notes, which tell you what there is on each major research subject.

Before you go it is well worth doing as much research as you can to identify which specific archive you want (is it actually there?), and pick out two or three strands you can work on.

This is especially necessary as, even once you are there in person, you will have to wait while the records you have requested are delivered to you. Early morning may be the best time to get results quickly, as the system slows when more people arrive.

As a result you should expect to achieve fairly little on your first visit to the Public Records Office. If you are travelling to London specially, do allow for plenty of time in Kew or you will almost certainly come away frustrated at how little you have achieved.

www.pro.gov.uk
This is the PRO's own website, which you clearly need to consult in considerable detail to get a picture of what records are, and are not, there. Many of the resources you want to consult may now be at the Family Records Centre instead, though the PRO record holdings remain vast and hugely valuable.

PROCAT introduces the catalogue of holdings (over nine-million files) and, within that area of the site, Information Leaflets is another area that you will undoubtedly find exceptionally useful.

www.pro.gov.uk/about/visit.htm
This URL shortcuts you to a visit-planning area of the website. If you scroll to the very bottom of this page and click on 'planning your visit' you will reach a detailed page of 'Useful Information for Visitors.'

You are now as well-equipped as you will ever be, so we hope that even your first attempt at grappling with the massive range of documents and resources held here will prove richly rewarding.

others who will do research for you

There are going to be times, however assiduously you are able to pursue your own research, when it is difficult for you to do it all unaided. At these moments, when a necessary document or reference is too far away to be conveniently visited, or some new avenue of research is being held up for lack of one vital piece of information, you could do with some help. Where do you turn?

The sources for finding researchers 'for hire', so to speak, are principally either in magazine advertisements, such as in *Family Tree Magazine*, or on the Internet. The same warnings must apply to both, namely that you should seek assurances that the researcher in question is qualified to do the research and is not going to spin out the process to charge you a large fee.

Often, you can agree to pay in instalments, with the option of terminating the arrangement at any stage. Or, you can agree a top limit, either in terms of hours or cost. You can renegotiate when you see how well done the research being done on your behalf is going.

One other way of possibly finding a local researcher who will do work on your behalf is to contact the County Record Office in the relevant area. They tend to have records of local experts.

www.pro.gov.uk/research/irlist/default.htm

The Public Record Office cannot carry out research on your behalf but it does make this page available, linking to a number of researchers who have approached the PRO offering their services. One convenience is that you can search by topic, linking to a list of researchers who specialise in that particular subject. Many of the individual researchers can be contacted by email.

www.users.dircon.co.uk/~searcher

Public Record Searches are offered here by Bob O'Hara, who actually lives in Kew, so is well-placed to visit the PRO. His areas of expertise are Army, Navy, Merchant Navy, Air Force, Police and Foreign and Colonial Office records.

www.one-name.org

The Guild of One-Name Studies, known as GOONS, are prepared to help with your research where they can, though they all do it voluntarily, so don't expect miracles time-wise. They also have access to 'Soldiers Died in the Great War', a CD database compiled from the 81 volume book published in 1921, and are prepared to perform look-ups for GOONS members.

www.agra.org

The Association of Genealogists and Researchers in Archives was formerly the Association of Genealogists and Record Agents. No matter, they still list those members available for commission and explain the various skills they can offer. The fact that they have all met certain standards of competence and comply with the AGRA code of practice gives you some assurance as to their reliability. Their website is somewhat primitive in appearance but the service is a good one.

www.asgra.co.uk

The Scottish Association of Genealogists and Record Agents is effectively the Scottish equivalent of AGRA, but with a much more up-to-date website.

www.achievements.co.uk

Achievements of Canterbury is the oldest genealogical research organisation of its kind. Professionally staffed by researchers who have been trained by the Institute of Heraldic and Genealogical Studies, you should find its services reliable.

www.ukbdm.org.uk

The UK BDM Exchange, run by Graham Pitt, is a wonderful co-operative resource, in the sense that it is essentially a swapping service for vital records. To explain how it works you need to scroll down the left-margin index, to the 'Help' button and then go to 'About' at the bottom of the page.

support for getting over difficulties

This chapter could easily fill a whole book, since there are so many ways in which the problems that face the family history researcher can be addressed. The first thing to remember is that it is more important to know where to find out information than to have vast reams of personal knowledge at your disposal. It is important to make use of the great data resources available, whether in libraries or the Internet, which is after all a virtual library itself.

Real-world libraries are probably not a mystery to you – the Internet may be. If so, you are not alone. Very few people have a sound knowledge of how it works or how to find their way around.

The most important method of doing so is to use a good search engine. This is always going to be a matter of preference and familiarity, though if you have not made your selection already we advise **www.google. co.uk** as being the most helpful.

If you are searching for UK records, do use the '.co.uk' version of Google, not '.com' because it offers you the chance to restrict your search to the UK and thereby to cut down spectacularly on the numbers of websites offered in answer to each request.

Do also use your imagination when instructing search engines. Search engine robots, or 'spiders', have no imagination so they are dependent on yours.

You may be looking for military records from the nineteenth century, for example.

So, if things are getting really sticky try a whole host of even vaguely relevant words, such as 'army, soldiers, fighting, service records, Victorian, Boer War, Crimea, battles' and so on. Google will deliver the results within seconds (indeed usually inside one second), so the initial stage of the search process is a very quick one.

www.joesgenealogy.com

Joe's Genealogy is a website to turn to when all else fails and you are getting frustrated. Joe Houghton has lots of personal experience and puts it across in a very practical way. There are no special instructions for using this website; simply explore.

www.tcwaters.free-online.co.uk

Ibertek is another multi-purpose, multi-problem-solving genealogy gateway, handled by T.C. Waters of Whitby in North Yorkshire. If that makes it sound small-scale and provincial, think again. It is massive, impressively well-organised and will keep you happy for hours.

www.friendsreunited.com.uk

Friends Reunited is one of those blissfully simple ideas for which the Internet seems made. They claim that over 20,000 people sign up every day, hoping to make contact with school, college or university friends – and now, in addition to the records of 40,000 academic institutions, they have recently added 400,000 workplaces.

www.salvationarmy.org

The Salvation Army will help you find missing persons, such as long-lost relatives, though it is not a service for putting adopters or adoptees in touch.

http://freebmd.rootsweb.com

Free BMD is held within the American website, Rootsweb. It is an admirable idea, making civil registration records available online. Over 30-million records have been transcribed in this way.

www.treeprint.co.uk/index.htm
TreePrint provides a printing service for those who want to store their family tree in hard-copy form, whether on parchment-style scrolls or large-page formats, without having to spend hours printing them out on separate pages and sticking them together.

www.gensuck.com
When you've got really fed up with surfing the Net and getting nowhere, Gensuck's rants will at least make you feel you are in good company!

latin

Did you learn Latin at school? If you did then you have a definite advantage when it comes to family history research. If you didn't, don't panic, you don't need to sign up for the nearest GCSE course and start learning Latin from scratch.
You may find that you actually do know more Latin terms than you think (*in situ*, *vice versa*, *ad hoc*, *modus operandi* and so forth). If you do want to follow a course you would do better to look for one in palaeography (reading old documents) rather than specifically in Latin.

In the UK, Latin was always a language of formal use only, but long after it had ceased being employed for even this purpose, it continued to be used for record-keeping and legal documents.

Those creating such documents, however, were not always educated to the highest level. Many clerks learnt the Latin terminology parrot-fashion and simply copied it without any syntactical understanding, so the family historian is often confronted with a poor version of Latin in the first instance.

Also, the same terms recur time and time again. So, when your first stumbling attempt to read the will of an early ancestor, for example, seems agonisingly slow, remember that the words are almost certainly following a well-worn formula – one you will soon come to know very well.

Michael Gandy has written a small booklet called 'A Basic Approach to Latin for Family Historians', available through your local Family History Society. Two other useful books are J. Cornwall's *Reading Old Title Deeds* and E. Gooder's *Latin for Local Historians*. For further books and leaflets on the topic, see:

www.ihgs.ac.uk/bookshop/bookshop_browser.php?cat=08
The Institute of Heraldic and Genealogical Studies bookshop has a 'palaeography and Latin' page. You need to scroll to the right to see the prices.

Meanwhile, the big genealogy websites, like **www.familysearch.com** and **www.cyndislist.com** have links offering help. Other possibilities are:

www.bbc.co.uk/history/lj/locallj/getstarted_03.shtml
The BBC's History Trail has an article to encourage you, entitled 'Getting Started' by Dr Alan Crosby.

www.quicklatin.com
Quick Latin is a translator from Latin to English, which you can try out for free and then subscribe to if you like it.

http://kufacts.cc.ukans.edu/ftp/pub/history/Europe/Medieval/aids/latwords.html.
University of Kansas Latin Word List.

www.georgetown.edu/irvinemj/classics203/resources/latin.lex
The Hard Little Words, a page of Latin prepositions and conjunctions.

www.uklegal.com/articles/latin.htm
UK Legal offers a Glossary of Latin Terminology that is one of the best for words or phrases to be found in legal documents.

glossaries of unfamiliar terms

You will encounter some unfamiliar words or phrases at some stage of your research. These websites might help. They are not the only ones, so try Google if you don't solve it here.

If you prefer to have a book on your desk, rather than have to use the PC as your route to the glossary you want, you probably need Joy Bristow's *The Local Historian's Glossary of Words and Terms*. The 3,000 terms it covers deal with some Latin terms and phrases, British currencies over the centuries, weights, measures and Roman numerals, and the tricky problem of regnal years.

www.genuki.org.uk/big/Occupations.html
GENUKI, the habitual 'bible' for the family historian, looks at occupations, with half a dozen onward links on offer.

www.gendocs.demon.co.uk/trades.html
Gendocs also lists unusual terms for professions and trades, all the way from able seaman to zoographer.

www.scan.org.uk/researchrtools/ glossary.htm
A List of Occupations covers similar ground to the above, but starts with 'Acater'.

http://homepages.nildram.co.uk/ ~jimella/acronyms.htm
Genealogical Acronyms and Glossary provides a useful short list.

www.scan.org.uk/researchrtools/ glossary.htm
Research Tools is a glossary to the Scottish language as used in early documents.

www.sog.org.uk/prc/abbr.html
The Society of Genealogists presents a list of Parish Register Copies: Abbreviations, partly those used in its

own records and partly those for religious denominations, which makes this an almost indispensable list.

dates, calendar changes and regnal years

As civilisations evolved they had to develop some form of calendar, but nature failed to help. There is not a perfect match between calendars based on the length of a day, a year or a lunar month. And which day is the first of the year?

The Romans created an accurate calendar, the Julian, with the year beginning on 1 January. Early English chroniclers preferred to start on Christmas Day, and from the late twelfth-century England adopted the continental habit of starting on Lady Day (25 March, the Feast of the Annunciation, nine months before Christmas). However, some scholars, especially Benedictines, continued to use Christmas Day.

In 1582 Pope Gregory ordered reform, and certain European countries (and Scotland from 1600) agreed to begin the year on 1 January. As a result, the period between 1 January and 24 March was sometimes given a double date (e.g. Charles I was executed on 30 January 1648/9).

Lord Chesterfield's 1751 Act finally replaced the Julian calendar with the Gregorian calendar in England and omitted the 11 days between 2 September and 14 September 1752. This is why the Inland Revenue tax year starts on 5 April.

The taxman was not going to give up any days, so his year had to start 11 days after 25 March. The rest of us just lost the days.

Europe in general followed suit but the Eastern Orthodox Church did not acknowledge the Pope, and so Greece, the Balkans and Russia did not introduce these changes.

While all this business may seem rather obscure and overly complicated, it can actually be of extreme relevance to family historians.

Rather than understanding how to work out dates in detail, the solution is to have a good reference work to hand, which will help you calculate dates before 1752 correctly. A suitable one for this purpose is *Dates and Calendars for the Genealogist* by C. Webb.

Alternatively, you may prefer to use the following website:

http://freepages.genealogy.rootsweb.com/ ~engregisters/registers/readnumbers.htm #1752
The 1752 Calendar Change, as explained within Rootsweb.

regnal years

If the calendar change seems tricky enough to understand, Regnal years are even worse. They were the original style of defining dates of an occurrence; for example, 'in the sixth year of the reign of King...'. This form was used in ancient Egypt, and has been used until recently in Britain, in a legal context, for Acts of Parliament.

A Regnal year dates from the day of succession, which is the day following the death of the previous sovereign (not the date of the new monarch's coronation), and so do not match the calendar year. Thus, Regnal years for Her Majesty Queen Elizabeth II start on 6 February, although she was not crowned until June.

The one exception to the above is William I, the Conqueror. It obviously took time to establish an invading King's rule as King of England, and so his Regnal year did begin at his coronation. This was on

Christmas Day 1066 at Westminster Abbey, when he was crowned by Aldred, Archbishop of York. The battle of Hastings had happened more than two months earlier, on 14 October.

http://freepages.genealogy.rootsweb.com/ ~engregisters/registers/readnumbers.htm #regnal
Regnal Years are explained here, again from within the Rootsweb website.

old handwriting

All family historians come across the problem of deciphering difficult handwriting at some stage. It may arise from a number of causes, not only the poor skill of the original writer. Documents stain and deteriorate easily, sometimes becoming extremely creased, sometimes having their top surface eroded, therefore leaving only partial traces of what was originally written.

There are, however, some things you can do that will help you decipher them. Whenever you encounter an unreadable word, you should seek out another part of the text that is more legible.

Most writers form their letters in a consistent manner, so you need to learn the handwriting quirks of the writer in question. Also, many documents of the sort you are likely to be reading, such as title deeds to land or wills, are likely to use stock phrases and repetitive formulae, so pressing ahead fairly quickly on your first attempt may be helpful, even if you go back to fill in the earlier details.

You should also try to familiarise yourself with styles of handwriting at different historical periods, and also with some of the shorthand-like abbreviations that were used by scribes in a hurry.

A medieval hand will be very different from a nineteenth-century one, yet once you know some of the conventions of medieval orthography the earlier hand may not be the more difficult.

For example, one of the most confusing habits of eighteenth- and nineteenth-century letter writers was to save paper by writing first across the page in the normal manner and then at right angles to the original script, writing over the top. Until you get used to this, the chaotic appearance of the result can seem an insurmountable obstacle to decipherment.

Booklets on this topic can probably be obtained through your local Family History Society. The Internet offers some online tutorials at **www1.freebmd.org.uk/handwriting.html**

http://ourworld.compuserve.com/homepages/dave_tylcoat/handwrit.htm
This page presents Early English Handwriting from Dave Tylcoat.

http://amberskyline.com/treasuremaps/oldhand.html
Deciphering Old Handwriting by Sabina J. Murray.

structure of surnames and their meanings

In the beginning we all had a name, and one was enough. However, as we left our settled family groups or small villages where we had been known all our lives, a further distinguishing definition became necessary.

Second names, or 'sur'names (names on top) were created to better define an individual, and the easiest is to say who you are the son of – Johnson, Wilson and so on.

There are other ways of naming a son after his father, such as the 'ap' in early Welsh (Owen ap Griffith) and 'mac' in Gaelic.

The next definition that was often used for identification in a large village depended on personal attributes – Black, Strong or Wise. Less obvious ones include Blunt (derived from blond) and Henty (a form of 'Hendy' and middle English for polite or courteous).

The final 'local' definition is the trade a person followed. Any name ending in 'er' or 'man' is likely to indicate this etymology, such as Chapman, an itinerant seller of books; Fletcher, a maker of arrows; Wainwright, a maker of farm carts; or Bridgeman, a taker of tolls at a bridge.

Once people started moving around, their place of origin was obviously of significance. This provides perhaps the largest source of second names.

Any name ending in 'ton' (for example, Worthington) or 'by' (for example, Danby) probably indicates a place-name derivation. Place-names can themselves reveal the history of the place. A name ending in 'by' is of Scandinavian origin, as 'bú' is old Norse for a homestead. Therefore, such places are mostly found in the north of England.

The southern equivalent is 'ton', from the Saxon 'tún', also a homestead. Celtic names are mostly preserved in Cornwall and the west, particularly in river names.

Returning to surnames, however, there remain many that are not included in the major groupings above.

Much of the bird world is represented in names like Sparrow, Partridge and Pigeon (though not the animal world, apart perhaps from very few, such as Fox and Wolf). Had the holders of these names caught or kept those birds, perhaps, or did they resemble them?

Remember that spellings were fluid, so as you move back in time expect to find yourself in some strange places in the index. For example, Paycock was an early form of Peacock, but Peecock, Pokoc and Pecok have all been seen.

There are many dictionaries of names on the market. Good early ones include *A Dictionary of English and Welsh Surnames* by Bardsley, printed in 1901 and reprinted in 1980, and *British Family Names* by Barber, printed in 1903.

The risk of some of the many modern publications is that they have tried to latch on to the current interest in genealogy, and are, to put it kindly, far from authoritative. Some titles recommended by reputable websites, however, are *Dictionary of English Surnames* by P.H. Beaney and R.M. Wilson, *Discovering Surnames* by J.W. Freeman and *The Surname Detective* by Colin D. Rogers.

www.familytreefind.co.uk/pink.htm#origin ates

This is the Pink family website but, if you connect to this specific page, you will find a feature about the origins of the Pink name prefaced by a very good article explaining the derivation of names in general. Topics covered are How a Surname Originates, What Does it Mean and Spelling Variations.

http://freepages.genealogy.rootsweb.com/ ~engregisters/registers/latinnames.htm
http://freepages.genealogy.rootsweb.com/ ~engregisters/registers/realnames.htm

Latin Names and Abbreviations and Real Names and Abbreviations consecutively. These two pages, hosted under the Rootsweb umbrella, are especially useful for identifying what full names can be assumed from standard abbreviations.

addresses

The British Library
96 Euston Road
London NW1 2DB
tel: 020 7412 7000

The British Library
Newspaper Library
Colindale Avenue
London NW9 5HE
tel: according to department

Corporation of London
Library and Art
Gallery (COLLAGE)
PO Box 270
Guildhall
London EC2P 2EJ
tel: 020 7606 3030
email: pro@corpoflondon.
gov.uk

Family Records Centre
1 Myddelton Street

London EC1R 1UW
census and general
enquiries: 020 8392 5300
births, marriages, deaths:
0151 471 4800
fax: 020 8392 5307

Federation of Family
History Societies
The Benson Room
Birmingham and Midland
Institute
Margaret Street
Birmingham B3 3BS
tel: 01704 149 032
email: admin@ffhs.org.uk

General Register Office
PO Box 2
Southport
Merseyside PR8 2JD
general information:
0151 471 4800
certificate ordering:
0151 471 4816

email: certificate.
services@ons.gov.uk

General Register Office
for Scotland (GROS)
Room 1/1/1,
Ladywell House,
Ladywell Road,
Edinburgh EH12 7TF,
tel/email: according to
department

The Guild of One-Name
Studies
Box G
14 Charterhouse Buildings
Goswell Road
London EC1M 7BA
email: guild@one-
name.org

Guildhall Library
Aldermanbury
London
EC2 2EJ

tel: *manuscript section*
020 7332 1863
email: manuscripts.
guildhall@corpoflondon.
gov.uk
maps and prints:
020 7332 1839
printed books:
020 7332 1868/1870
email: printedbooks.
guildhall@corpoflondon.
gov.uk
bookshop: 020 7332 1858
fax: 020 7600 3384

Historical Manuscripts
Commission
Quality House
Quality Court
Chancery Lane
London WC2A 1HP
tel: 020 7242 1198
fax: 020 7831 3550
email: nra@hmc.
gov.uk

LDS Distribution Centre
399 Garretts Green Lane
Birmingham B33 0UH
tel: 0121 785 2200

London Metropolitan
Archives
40 Northampton Road
London EC1R 0HB
tel: 020 7332 3820
fax: 020 7833 9136
email: ask.lma@corpof
london.gov.uk

National Archives of Ireland
The National Archives
Bishop Street
Dublin 8
tel: + 353 (1) 407 2300
fax: + 353 (1) 407 2333
email: mail@national
archives.ie

National Statistics *see*
General Register Office

The Public Record Office
Kew
Richmond
Surrey
TW9 4DU
tel: 020 8392 5200
fax: 020 8392 5286

Public Record Office for
Northern Ireland (PRONI)
66 Balmoral Avenue
Belfast BT9 6NY
tel: (+44) 028 90 255905
(Public Search Room)
fax: (+44) 028 90 255999
email: proni@dcalni.gov.uk

The Society of Genealogists
14 Charterhouse Buildings
Goswell Road
London EC1M 7BA
tel: 020 7251 8799
fax: 0207 250 1800
email: genealogy@
sog.org.uk

index